FAMILY ASSESSMENT

SAGE HUMAN SERVICES GUIDES, VOLUME 33

SAGE HUMAN SERVICES GUIDES

a series of books edited by ARMAND LAUFFER and published in cooperation with the University of Michigan School of Social Work.

A **SAGE** HUMAN SERVICES GUIDE **33**

FAMILY ASSESSMENT
Tools for Understanding and Intervention

Adele M. HOLMAN

*Published in cooperation with the University of
Michigan School of Social Work and Center for Social Work
and Applied Social Research, Fairleigh Dickinson University*

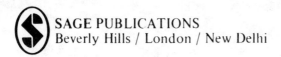 **SAGE** PUBLICATIONS
Beverly Hills / London / New Delhi

For information address:

SAGE Publications, Inc.
275 South Beverly Drive
Beverly Hills, California 90212

SAGE Publications India Pvt. Ltd.
C-236 Defence Colony
New Delhi 110 024, India

SAGE Publications Ltd
28 Banner Street
London EC1Y 8QE, England

Printed in the United States of America

Library of Congress Cataloging in Publication Data

Main entry under title:

Holman, Adele M.
  Family assessment.

  (Sage human services guides; v. 33)
  Bibliography: p.
  1. Family social work—United States. 2. Child abuse—Services—United States.
3. Foster home care—United States. I. Title. II. Series.
HV699.H57 1983   362.8'2   83-4514
ISBN 0-8039-2020-2 (pbk.)

FOURTH PRINTING, 1986

CONTENTS

PREFACE

This book has been developed as part of the Development and Delivery of Family-Centered Child Welfare Continuing Education Program by the Center for Social Work and Applied Social Research of Fairleigh Dickinson University. The project and the Family Assessment Guide owe much to the contributions of Ann Hartman. Through her influence as a teacher, consultant, and author of many published works, including *Finding Families,* she has had a major impact on human - service practice. Together with her colleagues at project CRAFT and the National Center on Adoptions, both at the University of Michigan, a framework for assessment was developed which utilizes the ecomap, the genogram, and family sculpture. As a result, family practitioners throughout the United States and Canada are using these assessment methods. This volume is an attempt to make this material even more available and accessible to a greater number of practitioners, particularly those who work with families where there are problems of child neglect and abuse.

With an emphasis on permanency planning as a guiding principle for child welfare service delivery, the focus on the Fairleigh Dickinson University project incorporates aspects of all three outcome areas: preventing unnecessary placement by strengthening family life, restoring children to their parents as

Author's Note: This book was developed as part of the Family Centered Child Welfare Project, Center for Social Work and Applied Social Research of Fairleigh Dickinson University, Barbara Bielawski, Project Director. The project was funded by the Administration for Children, Youth and Families, Office of Human Development, Department of Health and Human Services (Grant 02CT00010080).

promptly as possible when placement is required, and freeing children to become permanent members of another family when they cannot return to their own family. The concept of permanency planning grew out of the recognition that far too many children were being moved from one home to another as a result of short-range solutions. While such solutions met the need of the immediate problem, a great many children were not provided with the stable, long-term environment which would have fostered feelings of protection and security. Family assessment is viewed as a critical element in the process of determining realistic goals and effective interventions to meet these goals.

Much of the discussion on the assessment of families is drawn from experiences of practitioners concerned with permanency planning. However, while it is intended for use in mental health agencies, schools, public and private child welfare agencies, it can easily be adapted by a wide range of human service workers and students for use with other populations. The assessment framework is applicable to work with the aged, in health care settings, with the developmentally disabled, in industry, and with problems of substance abuse.

The purpose of this volume is twofold:

(1) To provide a conceptual framework for the assessment of families within an ecological perspective;
(2) To describe effective methods that can be used in the assessment process.

This guide addresses such questions as: What is the scope of family assessment? Why is it important? How is family assessment carried out? It also presents concepts of family functioning so that workers can become more skillful in assessing families.

Family assessment in this volume is approached from the point of trying to understand functioning of families in terms of

(1) the family as a system,
(2) the family and its environment,
(3) the life cycle of the family.

This guide also can be used independently in the classroom and in agency training programs, since case vignettes are used to illustrate theoretical concepts throughout the text. Additionally, it can be used as a manual in conjunction with the videotape *Family Assessment: An Approach to Child Neglect and Abuse,*[1] the script of which is found in Chapter 6. The videotape portrays two illustrative case situations that are typical of those confronting workers. Each of these is followed by a conference with experienced social workers discussing the case.

The first interview depicts a mother who requests foster placement for her child because she feels inadequate in coping with her. The second interview depicts a situation involving suspected child abuse in which the social worker has an exploratory meeting with the child's grandparents. Each interview raises questions for the worker in relation to how to reach a decision that will serve the best interests of the child and its family. Following the interview, a case conference, simulated by staff members of the Family Counseling Service of Hackensack, New Jersey, shows how significant issues are considered in the practice situation.

The two family interviews are four minutes and seven minutes in length, respectively. The discussions are fifteen minutes and eleven minutes. There is an opportunity for each segment to be used independently.

This guide represents the work of many people whose contributions should be acknowledged: Dr. Gene Webb, Director of the Center for Social Work and Applied Social Research at Fairleigh Dickinson University, for his guidance and cogent suggestions as a member of the Project Planning Committee; Professor Barbara Bielawski, Project Coordinator, with responsibility for Continuing Education; Professor Anita Weinberg, Project Curriculum Specialist, who supervised the filming of the videotape; Susan Koch Friedman, MSW, casework supervisor at the New Jersey Division of Youth and Family Services, Hackensack, New Jersey, who helped with the development of the videotape.

The following professional staff members of the Family Counseling Service, Hackensack, New Jersey, participated in simulated case conferences in the videotape: Gloria Warshaw, MSW, ACSW, Executive Director; Tricia De Bartolome, MSW, ACSW, Therapist and Supervisor; Ellie Amel, MSW, ACSW, Therapist and Supervisor; Janice Zarrow-Korenblatt, MSW, Therapist and Supervisor. In addition, Ms. De Bartolome helped in developing curriculum and she and Mrs. Zarrow-Korenblatt served as instructors for an in-service training course in family assessment offered to the staff of the Division of Youth and Family Services, Hackensack, New Jersey.

Anna Lascurian, Kristina Krasnow, and Joyce Rutledge, senior social work students, deserve thanks for performing in the interview segments of the videotape. Mary Stewart and Peter Carew, professional actors, also performed in the second interview segment.

Special thanks go to Dottie Ganzenmuller and Maria Capuano who typed the manuscript so capably and who were available for a myraid other tasks.

Teaneck, N.J.   Adele M. Holman, D.S.W.

NOTE

1. The videotape can be obtained separately from the Center for Social Work and Applied Social Research, Fairleigh Dickinson University, Teaneck, NJ 07666.

Chapter 1

THE USES OF FAMILY ASSESSMENT
Introduction

Parents who are secure, valued, and in control of their lives
are more effective parents than those who feel unsure and who
are not in control. Parents still have primary responsibility
for raising children, but they must have the power to do so in
ways consistent with their children's needs and their own
values. If parents are to function in this role with confidence,
we must address ourselves less to the criticism and reform of
parents themselves than to the criticism and reform of
institutions that sap their self-esteem and power. Recognizing
that family self-sufficiency is a false myth, we also need to
acknowledge that all today's families need help in raising
children.

—Kenneth Keniston and
the Carnegie Council on
Children (1977)

Caseworkers and other human service practitioners are
frequently faced with making decisions that have critical
consequences for clients and their families. When confronted
with problematic situations, they must decide upon interventions
which have serious and long-lasting implications. Therefore,
it is important that they base their decisions upon a

thorough understanding of how a family operates as a system and upon the knowledge gained from a comprehensive family assessment.

While the principal examples in this guide are drawn from practice with families where child neglect or abuse is the problem, the framework for assessment discussed also may be used in a broad range of human service work with troubled families. The following are some examples of situations where the family system concepts and family assessment tools can be appropriately applied to work in other areas of practice.

(1) A geriatric caseworker must decide, in the case of a client who had been seriously malnourished and is now ready for discharge, whether to recommend return to the family home where the condition developed or to recommend retention in the geriatric facility.

(2) The mental health practitioner in a psychiatric hospital who is preparing for deinstitutionalization of an emotionally disturbed client must assess whether the client's family is likely to provide a supportive environment or whether to recommend referral to a transitional residence.

(3) The social worker in a residential treatment setting is faced with the decision regarding whether the family of a rebellious adolescent can cope with her provocative behavior or whether a group home is a more suitable choice.

(4) The worker in a center for the developmentally disabled is confronted with a situation involving a marginally functioning young adult who is considered ready for return to the community. The question of whether the client's family has the capacity to deal with the frustration of caring for him or whether a foster home would be preferable must be answered.

(5) A school social worker is asked by a teacher to see a child who claims that her parents' excessive drinking and arguing interfere with her ability to concentrate on her homework.

(6) An employee assistance counselor meets with a worker who is depressed and whose work performance has seriously deteriorated. The worker complains of "family problems."

(7) A medical social worker has a diabetic patient whose failure to take prescribed medication and follow a prescribed diet has

resulted in considerable loss of vision. Circulatory problems have also developed and unless diet and medication are responsibly supervised within the family, serious complications are likely to result.

(8) A public assistance worker is concerned that a client family has frequent emergency requests and appears to be extremely disorganized.

In all of the above illustrations it is clear that undertaking a family assessment would furnish the worker with useful information. These data would then provide the basis for planning interventions to meet the needs of the clients and their families. In this guide, I will be drawing heavily on experience in the use of assessment techniques in working with families that have neglected or abused children. You will readily see that the concepts and techniques that are described for dealing with cases of child neglect and abuse can be transposed for use in one's own area of practice. A number of exercises are provided that encourage the reader to engage in the process of making a family assessment, and these exercises are equally useful in any area of practice. The task of adapting this material to your own work situation offers the opportunity to become proficient in applying concepts that are generic to the human services. As a point of departure, let us begin by examining how family assessment might be used in permanency planning.

Issues in Permanency Planning

As a means of understanding the uses of ecological approaches to family assessment, consider problems faced by workers concerned with permanency planning. When facing problematic situations involving children who have been maltreated or endangered, the worker must decide whether it is necessary to seek alternatives to the normative living arrangements. Adopting the mandate that is implicit in permanency planning, attention must be focused on active decision-making about the best possible living arrangement for the child. To do this requires a family assessment that is as speedy and comprehensive as the situation allows.

It is important to determine, first, whether there is clear evidence of danger to the child or whether there is suspicion of danger that needs to be verified. The question is whether the situation requires prompt removal of the child from the family home or if the child can safely remain there while further assessment of the family is being carried out.

If the problem concerns a child who has already been removed from the home, family assessment must be undertaken to determine whether the situation is sufficiently improved so that the child can safely return to the family or whether the child must be continued in an alternative living arrangement. The outcome of the family assessment will prepare the worker in considering which of the possible alternatives is most appropriate.

If the assessment indicates that the family shows promise of improvement, it may be advisable to maintain the child in temporary care while work continues with the family. If, however, the family situation shows insufficient evidence of improved family functioning and there is reason to believe that the neglect or abuse will be continued, then a decision to move the child to a permanent out-of-home care arrangement is indicated. Before such action can be taken, good practice and the laws of states require that a minimum amount of time be available to the family to demonstrate if it can make needed changes. This time, the agency is expected to provide maximum assistance in an effort to remedy the neglect or abuse. In those situations where the family has been given time and assistance to remedy the neglect or abuse, but has been unable to do so, the comprehensive family assessment, with supporting evidence, may provide the agency with the basis for recommending to the court that parental rights be terminated. For the worker to reach any of these possible decisions, it is crucial to have as clear and comprehensive an understanding as possible of how the family functions as a system to meet the needs of the child. Employing an ecological approach to assessment, an evaluation must be made in terms of the family's environment and how resources can be mobilized to enhance the family's capacity to provide for the child.

Often workers face the problem of reaching decisions under circumstances where they must act quickly yet with precision.

Experience has shown that failure to act expediently may result in serious physical or emotional abuse, sometimes even death. Consequently, it is critical for the worker to be able to draw upon a body of theoretical knowledge and to know how to use appropriate assessment tools. Only then does it become possible to answer such questions as: is this a safe and protective family environment? Is it conducive to raising a child or is it chaotic? Does it meet the basic needs of the child for physical sustenance? Is it possible for the child to grow to become an emotionally stable person? Can the child learn to relate in a healthy way to family members as well as peers? Are there members of the extended family who can participate in child rearing? Are there resources available to the family that are being overlooked?

The worker who has made a skillful assessment should be able to provide tentative answers to these questions and prepare to make a realistic plan for intervention. It is only possible to arrive at more definitive answers after time has elapsed and a further assessment has taken place that examines old and new evidence. Then a determination can be made as to whether the interventions have been useful or whether alternative plans must be made.

Assessment

The worker who is confronted with the need to make a decision in a case of apparent neglect or abuse of the child, must promptly strive to understand what has been happening in the family and what circumstances have contributed to the neglect or abuse. Family assessment is, therefore, a crucial step in the problem-solving process.

What Is Assessment

Assessment consists of trying to understand what the problem is, what is causing or contributing to the problem, and what can be changed or modified (Hollis, 1972). It is the appraisal of the situation and the people in it on the basis of facts, feelings, persons, and circumstances (Brill, 1978). Lauffer (1982) perceives assessment within a broad perspective, as a way of examining what is (here-and-now assessment), what is likely to be (future-oriented assessment), and what ought to be (normative assessment). It is important for the assessment to be carried out in an efficient way, if the intervention is to be effective, because interventions that are unplanned or unfocused succeed only by chance, if they succeed at all (Popple et al., 1977).

The assessment process ideally should be carried out as a shared responsibility between the worker and the family. This approach can facilitate the gathering of the data that form the basis for the decisions to be made. It is not unusual, however, in permanency planning for workers to deal with a family that is uncooperative or even strongly resistant to sharing information.

In assessing families, Germain and Gitterman (1980) point out that both objective and subjective data are necessary. Objective data provide information about family membership, family roles, the physical living setting of the family, and family rules. Subjective data reflect personal reactions and meanings attributed to events and processes and, for family members involved, their feelings about people and events. From these data, tentative inferences can be made, and hypotheses can be tested against client feedback, outcomes of worker and client reactions, and their mutual interaction. Germain and Gitterman (1980) also feel that while connecting empirical data to knowledge and theory is the science of assessment, professional assessment must be compassionate and empathetic because only then can it be genuine and not a stereotypical assessment of the family.

Approaches to Assessment

Current approaches to permanency planning and other areas of human service practice reflect awareness of the profound responsibility that is inherent in the worker's decision-making role. The worker who undertakes the assessment of a family must measure the situation of the child and other family members against the prevailing standards of the community. In the area of child welfare, for example, contemporary community standards reflect attitudes that were promulgated first in the UN Declaration of the Rights of the Child in 1954 and later affirmed in 1970 by the White House Conference on Children. These standards include the right of children to have special protection; to enjoy opportunities and facilities that will enable them to develop in a healthy and normal manner; to enjoy the benefit of adequate nutrition, housing, recreation, and medical services; to grow up in an atmosphere of affection and security and, wherever possible, in the care and under the responsibility of their parents; to receive special education, treatment, and care; and, if handicapped, to be protected against all forms of neglect, cruelty, and exploitation (Kadushin, 1980).

Keniston (1977) stresses the concept that decisions relating to whether to remove a child from the home have the most serious lifelong consequences and should never be made without careful assessment. He recommends that "before any child is removed from the home, except for brief emergencies, it must be made clear that the child is in imminent danger of serious physical harm or of extreme psychological or emotional harm." In making the assessment, it is important to view the family as an interacting system whose members meet each other's needs in a variety of ways. Therefore, it is essential that the needs of children, as well as those of their parents be considered when an initial decision is being made that could involve removal from the home (Derdyn, 1977).

Human service workers who attempt to determine how to deal with cases of neglect or abuse of a child traditionally have assessed the characteristics and functioning of the mother. In a study of 100 families of neglected children who were being considered for placement, the decision was found to be based largely on evaluation of maternal care (Boehm, 1967). Approaches that make assumptions about parental behavior and the consequences for children often have been unsubstantiated and based upon narrow perspectives (Stein et al., 1978). An emphasis on pathology has often led to dealing with complex problems in an oversimplified manner. It is inferred that parents are not capable of fulfilling their responsibilities if they have serious problems. By contrast, in an effective assessment, emphasis will be placed on the motivation and the commitment of the family to change. If there is evidence of commitment to change, the possibilities for strengthening the family are then explored. The level of demonstrated improvement and future prospects for change become criteria for making the decision as to whether it is necessary to remove a child or, once removed, to recommend return to the family. Are there other standards to consider when families deal with a disabled adult, an unemployed father, an aging parent, an alcoholic mother? What are they?

Adopting an ecological approach to family assessment, as proposed by Hartman (1979), acknowledges that families do not exist in a vacuum. There is recognition of "the sensitive balance that exists between families and their environment." This view provides a model for focusing on the family's strengths and assets as well as their deficiencies, and Hartman believes that an ecological approach offers a framework for understanding the transactional relationships between the family and its environment. Furthermore, this approach encourages a broad perspective in seeking resolutions of the perplexing dilemmas pertaining to permanency planning.

The complex ecological system consisting of a family and its environment is illustrated below in Figure 1.1.

It can be noted that the lines connect the Jones family with many other systems including friends, extended family, and formal organizations in their ecological field. The importance of the relationship between families and other systems in their environment is discussed later in the text.

Summary

Assessment is viewed as the appraisal of a problem based upon both objective data, or facts about the situation, and sub-

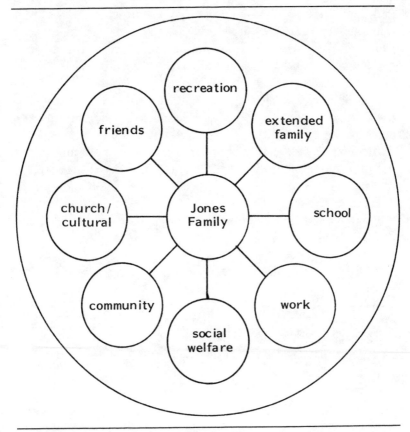

Figure 1.1

jective data, or feelings and reactions about the situation. To be genuine, assessment is compassionate as well as scientific. Community standards with respect to the minimal rights of children provide a measure for the practitioner to use in reaching critical decisions related to removal from, or return to, the family home. Motivation and commitment to change on the part of the family are criteria to be considered in this process. For an assessment to be comprehensive, the family is viewed from an ecological perspective investigating the balance between the family and its environment. This holds true whether working with child neglect and abuse or in other problem areas related to families such as mental health, substance abuse, aging, and health care.

Chapter 2

THE FRAMEWORK FOR FAMILY ASSESSMENT

There are four principal areas to be investigated in carrying out a family assessment. Knowledge of each of these areas is essential for the assessment to be a useful component in the problem-solving process. The four principal areas are

(1) the problem,
(2) the family as a system,
(3) the family and its environment,
(4) the family life cycle.

In this chapter we will deal with the first two items and then move on to environmental and life cycle concerns in Chapter 3. Both chapters should be read as a single unit.

The Problem

A clear understanding of the nature of the problem is essential in deciding how to deal with it. From an etiological point of view, the worker needs to know the duration of the problem. This is an important factor since chronic problems are harder to change than are crises or problems of recent origin (Dukette et al., 1978). Information from past records and data from collateral sources are essential for beginning the assessment. Some questions to be answered are, How did the problem come to the attention of the agency? Is it of an urgent nature? What was the initial response of the agency? Have other agencies been involved in this problem and, if so, what interventions have taken place?

George is a 7-year-old boy who appears to be much younger than his age. He is extremely withdrawn in school and is fearful of loud noises. His teacher has observed that he cringes when she speaks loudly or firmly to the class. He backs away when she leans down to show him something. The school social worker referred George to the Child Welfare Agency after his mother failed to keep three appointments to discuss the teacher's observations. The social worker feels that the family situation needs to be assessed in order to understand how to deal with George's difficulty in interacting with children and adults.

Questions raised by this case point to the complexity and duration of the problem as issues to be explored. Are there records of problems relating to George in any of the agencies that have provided services to this family? Examples of possible service agencies are the day care center, the health care agency, and the school in the neighborhood where George's family lived prior to this year. It also is essential to know how the parents view the problem. To what extent have they tried to deal with it and with what results? If other family members are involved, how do they react to it and do they explain it? Are they willing to work toward changing the situation? Has George been able to relate his view of the problem and, if so, how has he been able to deal with it? The more pervasive the problem, the less likely it is that it can be resolved without active outside intervention on the part of the agency.

The Family as a System

The family is generally perceived by society as the unit responsible for providing children with an environment that serves their physical and emotional needs (Goldstein et al., 1973). It is accepted practice today to view the family as a system organized around the support, regulation, nurturance, and socialization of its members (Minuchin, 1974). Within this framework, the family also can be viewed broadly as "a small social system made up of individuals who are related to each other sharing strong reciprocal affections and loyalties who comprise a household (or cluster of households) that persists over years. Members enter the family through birth, adoption, or marriage and leave only by death" (Terkelsen, 1980). In addition, children also enter a family by way of foster placement. Unique to this family group of people is its legal status in society (Odgen and Zevin, 1976). Family members can be described as depending upon each other for survival in many ways. This is true particularly for children who depend upon the family not only for sustenance, but for socialization and for transmitting the culture (Nye and Bernardo, 1973).

In general systems terms, the family can be perceived as a dynamic system consisting of a complex of elements or components (family members) directly or indirectly related in a network, in such a way that each component (family member) is related to some other in a more or less stable way within any particular period of time. The interrelationships of the family members create a whole (family) that is greater than the sum of its parts (Compton and Galaway, 1979). Within this context, the family is seen as a transactional system, in constant interchange with its extended environment and developing intergenerally through time (Hartman, 1979).

Minuchin (1974) viewed the family as a system of interacting parts, with the family system differentiating and carrying out its functions through subsystems. Individuals are the subsystems within a family. Subsystems can be formed by generation (parents, children); by sex (mother-daughter, father-son); by interest or abilities (swimmers, nonswimmers); or by function (father, mother, oldest child as caretakers).

A family consisting of parents, a son, two daughters, and a grandmother who live in the same household is illustrated in Figure 2.1. The connecting lines demonstrate the relatedness

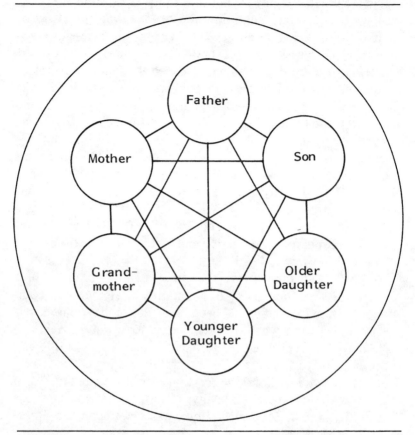

Figure 2.1

of each of the family members to each other. The outer circle is the boundary defining the family as a distinct group.

It is important to know that within a family there is a relationship among all family members. It is especially important to recognize the connections and to understand the implications of these connections. A change in any one member affects other individuals and the group as a whole.

When faced with a problem concerning the well-being of a child, systems theory focuses on the broad range of elements that affect the family, including their interrelationships and interdependencies. Any troubled family member may contribute to the situation directly or indirectly. Examples are an alcoholic mother, a father who cannot hold a job, an aggressive sibling, or an interfering grandmother. Troublesome behaviors create stresses that upset the balance of the family system, and, consequently, it is the total family system that must be the unit of attention for the whorker who is responsible for helping the child.

Boundaries

Within the systems framework, families can be said to have boundaries. These boundaries exist along a continuum from open (permeable), to partially open, to closed. A family with fully open boundaries can be described as accepting all members who wish to enter their system, as well as accepting all new ideas. This is in contrast with the closed family system that rigidly excludes all members but its own and rejects ideas that are discordant with its own views. Either extreme position can be a source of potential problems. The family that accepts all members will surely face a shortage of emotional, social, and material resources. Also, in failing to set limits to its membership, such a family may be failing to protect its members from exploitation.

> Marie, 13, is the oldest of six children fathered by four different men. Her mother encourages a steady stream of boyfriends in the household. She claims that she and her children could not subsist without the money and gifts that these men provide.
>
> Marie is sexually active and although her mother says that she disapproves, she buys her provocative clothing and does not supervise her activities. Marie ran away for a week with her 19-year-old uncle. Her 11-year-old sister told her classmates Marie had an abortion during that time.

In this family the excessively open boundaries have failed to protect Marie and the other children from exploitation by people outside the family.

At the opposite end of the spectrum is the closed family, which suffers from a lack of new ideas and of people whose entry would be appropriate (in-laws, close friends, community helpers, and the like).

Cassie is 14 years old, 5 feet tall, and weighs 155 lbs. Her mother is an isolated woman who does not permit Cassie or her siblings to go on school trips and discourages after-school contact with peers. She is resistant to requests to consider the social needs of her children. The home has no telephone and there is little contact with extended family members or members of the community.

Cassie is ridiculed by classmates for her obesity and slovenly appearance. Her mother refuses to discuss with the school nurse the health problems that Cassie is developing. She claims she doesn't want any interference from outsiders such as doctors or social workers.

Closed boundaries tend to exacerbate existing problems and prevent delivery of necessary stimulation and services.

Minuchin (1974) stresses the importance of clear boundaries within families. He is concerned that in some families excessive closeness and lack of differentiation of function develops, resulting in what he calls "enmeshment."

Joseph, 14, is observed by neighbors as his mother's constant companion. She waits for him to return from school so that he can accompany her to the supermarket, and he regularly helps her with household tasks. His father seems unconcerned about the overinvolvement between Joseph and his mother and Joseph's failure to develop autonomy appropriate to his life stage.

While it was functional in early childhood for a mother and son to be very closely involved, the enmeshment now tends to deter him from developing suitable interests, social skills, and sex-role identification.

The parents of Linda, 9, could not understand why she was so destructive at home and were referred for family counseling.

During the interview with the counselor, it was apparent that each time she directed a question to Linda, her father supplied the answer before she could respond. Linda was observed to become agitated whenever she was prevented from expressing herself.

When family members function for each other it prevents the development of self-differentiation. This is believed to be a significant factor in the failure of family members to think and act independently. If carried to an extreme, it often results in serious family problems (Bowen, 1978).

At the other end of the continuum of family boundaries is the family with inappropriately rigid boundaries, whom Minuchin terms "disengaged."

Peter, 13, is the only child of affluent parents who devote considerable time to their own concerns. His father is a busy surgeon and his mother is a regional tennis champion who is in frequent competitions. As Peter's behavior has become increasingly troublesome, school and community authorities have felt helpless to deal with the parents who each project blame for the problem onto the other. The mother and father have resisted becoming actively involved in assuming the duties that their parental roles require for the healthy development of their son.

In this disengaged family there is no responsible parent nor is there demonstrated concern for the problems of the child. Peter experienced a lack of relatedness to his family and there was a sense of isolation on the part of his parents until the juvenile justice agency intervened to confront them with the growing seriousness of their son's delinquent activities.

Disengaged families are characterized by functioning that is autonomous to such an extent that there is usually poor communication and lack of demonstrated concern. There may also be diminished family loyalties and unavailability in times of stress. This is in contrast to the enmeshed family, at the other extreme, where stressful behavior in one family member causes excessive reactivity in the others. (Minuchin, 1974).

Communication Patterns

Every family has its unique pattern of communication, with all members conveying information both verbally and nonverbally. Verbal communication refers not only to spoken words but to related sounds such as laughter, moans, grunts, as well as to inflection and tone of voice. Nonverbal communication, known as "body language," sends messages by means such as posture, facial expressions, and movements. Impressions about a person and a situation are thus conveyed simultaneously by processing the various types of communications.

Just as each person has a distinct style of communication, so too does a family have its own style of communication. Patterns showing who talks to whom about what tell a great deal about how the family operates in terms of attitudes and values. Parental expectations are conveyed by the choice of topics they discuss with each child. In some families, sex-linked attitudes and values reflect the functioning of the subsystems. This is shown when fathers mainly discuss sports with sons and mothers mainly discuss household matters with daughters. By contrast, in other families where boundaries are more open, topics may be freely discussed across lines of gender. Some families tend to be flexible and encourage casual conversations while others restrict conversation by setting a tone of disapproval if a topic is objectionable to a family member in authority. Unwritten rules about subjects that are approved or disapproved reveal much about a family and its taboos. In some families, financial issues may be discussed only between certain members, while in some families, sexual issues may not be discussed at all.

Unclear communications are believed to contribute to significant problems in family functioning if the pattern is repeated frequently. Simultaneous communications of conflicting messages may place a family member in a "double blind" with no clear way to gain approval. An example is an overt message to take an action coupled with a covert message implying that if the action is taken, disapproval will result.

For purposes of family assessment, it is important for the worker to observe and evaluate communication patterns by raising questions such as, Are messages clear? Are some family members excluded from discussion? Are some family members habitually linked to blame for family problems? Do one or more family members provoke anxiety by their communications? Are conflicting messages communicated resulting in a double bind? Are there family taboos?

Family Structure

The assessment of how a family system functions requires a knowledge of the family structure. The repeated interactions demonstrating how, when, and to whom the family members relate are descriptive of the family structure. (Minuchin, 1974). Its nature can be understood by examining the broad range of patterned sequences of behavior observable in the interactions between two or more family members. (Terkelsen, 1980). The sum total of all the family roles being played within a given family represents its structure (Duvall, 1977).

The term "role" refers to the socially expected behavior prescribed for a person occupying a place in a particular social system. (Biddle and Thomas, 1966). Within the family, the traditional or formal roles are assigned and expected to evoke behaviors that will meet the family needs. Family rules and strategies determine how tasks, responsibilities, and transactions are distributed and carried out among its members. Examples are the parent as caretaker or wage earner or the child as student or helper. Social norms provide guides for attitudes, feelings, and behaviors that are expected or prohibited for the individual fulfilling that role (Compton and Galaway, 1979).

In all families, informal or ascribed roles are assigned to members so that the social and emotional needs of the family are met. Many families do not know that they have ascribed roles to their members but, structurally, members can identify such special informal roles as peace-keeper or problem-solver. Such roles are sometimes assumed without the conscious awareness of the family, and can be recognized if members are questioned as to who keeps the peace or who figures out how to work out the problems. Examples of common informal family roles are hero, victim, scapegoat, jokester, good daughter/son, black sheep, rebel. In some families, while these ascribed roles may meet the family system's need for balance, a role with negative connotation may be destructive to the family member who bears it as well as to the family. In such cases where an individual or the entire family functions at a low level, it is important to assess why the structure of the system supports a negative role for one or more of its members.

The performance of roles is a significant indicator of how a family is functioning or can be expected to function under stress. In assessing the structure of a family, the worker must examine how roles are performed and whether or not they meet the needs of the family. Some questions to explore are, Who occupies the various family roles? Do role performers relate in such a way that there is complementarity? Are roles ambiguous and therefore overlapping or left unfilled? Is there felxibility in role performance so that, in times of crisis, adaptation can be expected? Are role performances congruent with the expectations of society? Do ascribed roles tend to label family members pejoratively and thereby inhibit development of self-esteem?

The following are examples of some case situations that reflect problems related to roles and their influence on family system functioning.

Larry, 12, was the youngest of four children in a family where it was openly discussed that he was not a wanted child. Labeled "the accident," he grew up feeling unloved and that all family problems were his fault. This was reinforced when his father was unemployed for a lengthy period of time and Larry was made to feel that if he had not been born his family would have been better able to manage. When he ran away and was picked p by the police five days later, his family was referred to the local family agency. The initial family interview clarified Larry's role as scapegoat in the family as a significant factor in his leaving home and his resistance to rejoining the family.

All families have informal roles, but troubled families are more likely to have members occupying such dysfunctional roles as victim or scapegoat. In many families, scapegoating is a means of shifting responsibility from the stronger members of the family to the one who is most vulnerable. It is important in assessing problematic families to examine the informal roles occupied by family members as a means of understanding the background of the problems.

It is commonly accepted that if role behavior conforms to the norms for a family, it usually elicits approval. Negative sanctions in the form of punishment are usually applied to discourage deviant behavior. Each family member constructs expectations about his or her role from the message sent by other family members.

Alice, 6, had many digestive upsets as a baby and often refused the food her mother offered her. At 3, a series of tests determined that she had a congenital digestive problem and required a diet of food that was different from that prepared for the rest of the family. Mealtime was typically a time of battles between Alice and her mother, who pressured her to eat all of the specially prepared food. When she entered school, the teacher observed that even on hot days Alice wore long-sleeved shirts and long pants. Investigation revealed evidence of both recent and healed bruises. Now, placed in a foster home, she cannot accept praise from her foster parents and calls herself "bad Alice." She says that she deserved to be beaten because she was a bad girl.

Explicit norms for a family typically pertain to eating habits; achievement expectations in school work; or socialized behaviors such as cleanliness, politeness, and work-orientation; or maintaining racial or ethnic identity. Implicit norms might pertain to family loyalty, the degree of rebelliousness tolerated, sexual behavior expected, and respect for another's possessions.

Enactment of family roles is carried out most effectively when there is clarity as to the expectations of the role. Ambiguity tends to create confusion and results in tensions and unfulfilled functions.

Mr. S. is trying to maintain the family household since he separated from his wife and she left the home. He and his sons, John, 15, and Tim, 13, are engaged in constant arguments because he feels that they will not carry out their share of responsibility for the cooking, cleaning, shopping, and other tasks.

John is often truant from school and the police have been called on several occasions when he has stayed away all night. He claims that he cannot seem to satisfy his father regardless of what he does at home because his father always wants something different.

In her meeting with the father and sons, the school social worker focused on defining the boundaries of the new roles in the absence of the mother. Several sessions were spent in clarifying the tasks to be done and in negotiating which of the three family members would undertake the various tasks, such as cooking, shopping, cleaning, laundry. As the roles were gradually realigned, tension decreased noticeably and John's functioning began to improve.

Role enactment that is congruent with the needs and expectations of society is usually less conflict-laden than when the behavior is deviant and fails to meet the family's needs. In the family where the father is away for prolonged periods of time, there may be incongruity in the role performance for the son if the mother fails to reinforce role-appropriate behavior.

Jimmy, 10, is the son of a merchant seaman and often does not see his father for several months at a time. In his father's absence, his mother tends to rely on him for companionship to a very great extent. Also, she insists that he help with decision-making in instances that demand judgment beyond realistic expectations for a child of his age. As he becomes frustrated and resentful, his behavior becomes overly aggressive.

This phenomenon of the "parental" child tends to develop when the one parent is absent and the remaining parent encourages the child to enact some of the role functions of the absent parent. In terms of family systems theory, such role incongruity may be understood as the system seeking balance by providing a replacement for the absent parent. Similarly, in some families, hierarchical boundaries are breached and role reversals take place with an underresponsible parent depending upon an overresponsible child. In assessing the family, it is important to understand how the child is affected by this role shift.

Family members occupy a variety of roles simultaneously, that is, a "role cluster." When there are conflicts between the demands of the roles, problems affect the family balance.

> Mr. C. is fulfilling the roles of husband, father, employee, and Little League coach. His work has recently required considerable overtime and he has frequently been unable to carry out his coaching duties. His son, Billy, 11, is distressed that when the team loses a game, the other parents and his teammates place much of the blame on his father. They call him a "no show."
>
> Mrs. C. encourages her husband's overtime work and feels that time spent with the Little League is unimportant to the family; that he is just playing "child's games." The arguments that take place between Mr. and Mrs. C. make Billy regret that his father ever volunteered to be the coach.

When role conflicts exist, the situation requires an assessment of the family's value system. How such conflicts are resolved will influence the functioning of the family.

Crisis situations often provoke the need for role shifts and new role enactments. Previously effective role patterns may be disrupted without warning and the family system becomes unbalanced (Perlman, 1961).

> Severe disability due to an accident prevented Mr. D. from working, and Mrs. D.'s tension regarding unpaid bills provoked loss of control with the two children, 3 and 4. When she found herself at the point of beating the younger child, she recognized her need to get help. A series of consultations with a social

worker resulted in a plan for her to try to work outside of the home and to place the children in a day care center.

Mrs. D. found that her job as a waitress provided sufficient income to supplement her husband's disability payments. It also provided a social outlet for her so that she felt less resentful of the demands that her husband and children placed upon her.

Flexibility of roles can be a measure of how well a family structure functions. Shifting responsibilities and developing new roles is an indication of the ability of a family system to adapt to the stress of crisis situations. The absence of flexibility is a warning signal that a family will have repeated problems in coping with unexpected stresses.

Cultural and ethnic norms strongly influence how roles are carried out within a given family system. Knowledge of differing values, customs, and traditions are important so that the caseworker can interpret whether role enactment in a given situation is appropriate.

Maria, 15, was teased by her classmates because she always went straight home from school dances with an older brother or sister who called for her. They labeled her "Miss Goody-Good." When Maria was caught stealing some hair ornaments from a local store, she explained to the juvenile justice officer that she wanted to show the others that she was not always so good. The worker to whom she was referred was able to relate to Maria's conflict about the cultural differences between her and her classmates. She tried to help Maria and her parents understand the effects of stress placed on her by following a code of behavior that was not the norm of her peers.

Vernon, 9, never knew his father but he called his mother's father "Daddy." They were very close and spent a lot of time together. When his teacher asked the children who didn't have fathers at home to ask their mothers whether they could join the Big Brothers program, she could not understand why Vernon showed no interest. He had difficulty in telling her that he felt he already had a father who also happened to be his grandfather.

In some cultures, traditional family roles are performed by family members who hold other roles simultaneously. The family system with an absent father is not necessarily deviant. Members of the extended family, such as a grandfather, uncle, or older brother, often perform the role of father surrogate without conflict. In such situations, children should not necessarily be considered deficient in fathering if the cultural factors are understood (Tucker, 1979).

In addition to examining role performance in assessing the structure of families, it is necessary to explore other aspects of the usual patterns of behavior. In dysfunctional families, such patterns often reveal that one or more members become the focus of attention, and remain so by displaying symptoms or negative behaviors. It is postulated that when there is considerable anxiety in a relationship between two people, a third, vulnerable person is drawn into the relationship to act as a buffer or distraction (Bowen, 1978). This family pattern of "triangulation" is typically observed where the marital relationship is poor and the common bond between the parents is their mutual concern with the problematic behavior of a child. A number of such parents who project excessive blame onto a child for negative behavior and who are unaware of their role in the continuing problem can be linked to child neglect or abuse.

The reader will recognize that the understandings of family assessment discussed here in terms of inappropriate role performances and dysfunctional patterns of behavior are relevant not only to the problems of child-focused families, but also to families with other types of problems. Suggested approaches to planning interventions to deal with these problems will be discussed in a later chapter.

Family System Exercise

This exercise provides an opportunity to reinforce learning about family systems. It may be used by human service workers who work in a variety of settings. Select a client family that you know well.

(1) List the members of the family system.

_____   _____   _____

_____   _____   _____

_____   _____   _____

(2) Identify the subsystems in this family by generation, sex, interests/abilities, and function.

_____   _____   _____

_____   _____   _____

_____   _____   _____

_____   _____   _____

(3) Evaluate the boundaries of this family system on a continuum ranging from open (1) to closed (10)._____

(4) Rate the functioning of this family system on a continuum ranging from enmeshed (1) to disengaged (10). _____

(5) Identify the family members according to their formal or assigned roles.

___	___	___
___	___	___
___	___	___

(6) Identify the family members according to their informal or ascribed roles.

___	___	___
___	___	___
___	___	___

Place a "+" next to any role designation that you believe supports the growth of the family member and a "−" next to any role designation that inhibits feelings of self-esteem.

(7) Are there role conflicts within this family? If so, explain.

(8) Is there ambiguity in any of the roles? If so, explain.

(9) Is role shift likely to take place in time of crisis? If so, explain.

(10) Are family roles congruent with social norms and the needs of society? Explain.

(11) Think of ways in which cultural influences affect role performances in the family. Give examples.

(12) Are there relationships in which the family projection process takes place? If so, explain.

(13) How has knowledge of family systems expanded your understanding of this family? Explain.

Chapter 3

THE FAMILY IN SPACE AND TIME

For an ecological assessment to be thorough, it must include, in addition to knowledge of the family as a system, knowledge of how the family relates to its environment and how it has developed over an extended period of time. These significant dimensions of the family provide a basis for learning about a family in depth. Continuing to use examples related to permanency planning, you will read about how to evaluate the essential elements in the family's environment. Later in the chapter, you will read about how the family life cycle provides a framework for assessment.

The Family and Its Environment

The family's relationship to its environment is a critical focus for assessment in cases of permanency planning. In using the ecological approach, the caseworker investigates how the family system is matched with its environment (Hartman, 1979). Is there an adaptive mutuality that exits between the family's needs and the resources in the environment? What sources of supports are there within the family and the environment? Does the family's relationship with the people and institutions in the environment promote growth and well-being or are there gaps resulting in significant unmet needs? These questions focus on the holistic point of view toward people and their environments.

It is important to have a clear understanding of the overall scope of the family's environment and recognize that it consists not only of concrete realities such as food, clothing, shelter, medical care, employment, physical safety, education, and recreation, but also includes social realities in terms of interpersonal relationships. The total environment is a complex set of interacting forces impinging simultaneously from many different directions and interacting with a complex set of forces from within the family (Hollis, 1972).

The environment of a family should be perceived within a broad context viewing both physical and social perspectives before decisions are made as to the ability of a family to provide adequately for its children. It is necessary to evaluate the extent to which the elements in the physical environment meet the family's needs. What is the condition of the home? Does it provide bare necessities? Does it provide comfort and convenience? What is the income level and how does it affect lifestyle, sense of adequacy, and self-worth? Does the school provide an environment that is conducive to learning? Are there suitable health facilities at a cost that the family can afford? Are there services available for a handicapped person?

In addition to meeting the needs of its members for livelihood, shelter, and protection, families have the additional function of connecting their members to the outer world of society and their culture (Germain and Gitterman, 1980). Ethnic identity, social class, and regional role factors influence standards of behavior, aspirations, and perceptions (Hollis, 1972). The functioning of the family as a system reflects the input from other social units, the extent to which it fits into the cultural mold, and the expectations of the larger system (Compton and Galaway, 1979).

The social network, another major dimension in assessing families, refers to the important people in the family's environment. These people provide the means for relatedness, identification, affirmation, socialization to belief systems, norms, and cultural values. Such people function as the natural helpers in a mutual aid system.

In understanding whether a family has adapted to its social environment, the following questions can be asked: Is there either overdependence or alienation from the extended family members? Does the family have a network of friends and coworkers who are supportive? Does the family conform to neighborhood standards or is it deviant? How does the family deal with an exploitative landlord? Can the parent intervene effectively to stop harassment of a child? Answers to questions such as these will help to determine whether the family is organized or disorganized and what level of opportunity they can provide for the well-being of the children.

Assessing the fit between a family and its environment raises questions about the capacity of the family to deal with social strains. Environmental resources are often underutilized by families who have not learned to find and use services that are available to fulfill their family's needs.

Henry P., 12, was midly retarded and in a special class at school. Although he was athletic, he spent most afternoons alone in his room since neighborhood boys ridiculed him and excluded him from their games. His divorced mother accepted his isolation until he began to act out his frustration by punching his hand into the walls of his room. She dealt with this by refusing to cook for such a "big, dumb, angry kid!!"

When he injured his hand by repeated angry punches and it required treatment at the neighborhood health center, the social worker there referred Henry's mother for counseling at the Association for Retarded Persons. That suggestion was rejected until the tensions were further heightened by Henry's continued wall punching and his mother's retaliation by refusing to prepare cooked food for him. Finally, after a second and more serious hand injury, the school social worker insisted that Mrs. P. get help for herself and Henry or said that she would have to report them to the child protection agency.

Mrs. P. met with the counselor at the Association for Retarded Persons and learned that the local "Y" was beginning a Saturday morning athletic program for developmentally disabled youngsters. She later found that the parents of the other children who participated in the program provided a mutual aid system for her and also provided her with an outlet to discuss her feelings about having a retarded child.

Neglectful or abusive families must be challenged to demonstrate their commitment to change by availing themselves of environmental resources. It is the responsibility of the community and agencies to provide adequate resources and to work for improvements when environmental resources are deficient. It then becomes the responsibility of the caseworker and the agency to link client families with the appropriate resources, including natural helpers. Also, it its important for the caseworker to follow through with encouragement to sustain the contact so that these families can provide a level of care that meets the standards of the community.

Ecological Exercise

This exercise is designed to help you adopt an ecological approach to family assessment. It will stimulate thinking about how a family is connected to its environment.

(1) Think about your own family system.

(2) Turn to page 39 and apply the questions in the text to your family.

(3) Next, think about the physical environment of your family in terms of the questions on the top of page 40.

(4) Now, think about your family's adaptation to its social environment. Answer the questions on page 41 with your family in mind.

(5) Are there physical or social resources in the environment that would enhance the functioning of your family? List them.

The Family Life Cycle

There is much to learn from the concept of the life cycle of the individual, and from the life cycle of the family as a means of understanding life stages and stage-appropriate life tasks. This framework is useful early in the assessment process in order to understand whether a problem of maltreatment is related to the normal stresses of adjustment to the life stage or whether it is related to other factors.

In 1950, Erikson identified eight stages in the life cycle of the individual and the normal psychosocial development tasks that characterize each stage (1963). These stages and the principal issues to be confronted in each stage are conceptualized in the following model:

(1) infancy: trust versus mistrust,
(2) early childhood: autonomy versus shame and doubt,
(3) play age: initiative versus guilt,
(4) school age: industry versus inferiority,
(5) adolescence: identity versus identity diffusion,
(6) young adulthood: intimacy versus isolation,
(7) adulthood: generativity versus self-absorption,
(8) senescence: integrity versus digust.

In each of these stages, there are specific tasks that create stresses in the individual as well as the family and sometimes help is required to deal with the problems that result. In those families where adaptation to the life stage of the individual and the family has not taken place, problems of a more serious nature are likely to develop.

Before Andy, the youngest of five children, entered kindergarten he was feeling a geat deal of stress. As his mother walked him to school, he heard her tell another mother of how glad she was that he would be away from her and in school so that every day, for at least those few hours, she could stop being a mother.

When the children began to enter the classroom, she pushed Andy ahead and was the first mother to be gone. Once inside he ran wildly around the classroom trying to leave because, he told the teacher, if he stayed at school, his mother would stop being a mother.

This mother and her child had not developed the capacity to adapt to their life stages, and as a result, the potential for school phobia and other problems is high. The mother's self-absorption was in conflict with the need of her son for maternal support during this period of adjustment to his new life stage.

Growing out of a strong interest in the life cycle of individuals, there has come significant interest in the life cycle of the family. Recognition that successful achievement of each member of a family is related to how each other family member achieves appropriate life tasks has led to the conceptualization that the family, as a whole, has developmental tasks.

Approaching an understanding of the family unit by relating the family life cycle to its stage appropriate developmental tasks provides a paradigm for evaluating how a family is meeting the expected requirements of society. It offers a means of assessing how a family is functioning in each life stage and as it moves from one stage to another. Whether it can accommodate the transitional phases without becoming disorganized or failing to meet the needs of its members reflects the family's strength or limitations and whether its role performances are appropriate. Does a marriage have the strength to adjust to the birth of a child? Do the parents have the flexibility to adapt to the needs of growing children? How does the family cope with the maturing adolescent's need for emancipation? Will the family support the young adult through the launching phase? Is the family supportive of its aged members and the demands that physical decline bring about? How does the family cope with death and bereavement?

Duvall, in 1950, first formulated the eight stages of family development and she later outlined stage-critical tasks. Her landmark work has been updated to reflect contemporary family data and mores (1977). By examining Duvall's schema (Table 3.1) for carrying out a family assessment, the worker will easily identify the life stage that the family occupies by selecting from among those listed in the column on the left. Next, the positions that the family members occupy are matched to the family's life stage (middle column). Finally, the tasks that Duvall has conceptionalized as critical for those family members at the various life stages are listed in the column on the right. As an example, the worker whose client family consists of a married couple who are husband and wife are expected at this life stage to establish a mutually satisfying marriage, adjust to pregnancy and the promise of parenthood and, also, fit into the kin network. If the family is at the childbearing stage, then the family members' positions are wife-mother, husband-father, infant daughter or son. For this family, the expected developmental tasks are "having, adjusting to, and encouraging the development of infants" and also "establishing a satisfying home for both parents and infants." As this chart provides for a life stage that corresponds to any family, the worker will find it applicable to all of the families requiring assessment. Applying this chart directly to practice, the understanding of what is expected at the family's life stage clarifies for the worker whether a family is meeting the expected needs of its family members and points the way to interventive processes.

Linking life stage and appropriate tasks, Neugarten (1976) points to "a socially prescribed timetable for the ordering of major life events; a time in the life span when men and women are expected to marry, a time to raise children, a time to retire."

TABLE 3.1 Stage-Critical Family Developmental Tasks Through the Family Life Cycle

Stage of the Family Life Cycle	Positions in the Family	Stage-Critical Family Developmental Tasks
(1) Married couple	Wife Husband	Establishing a mutually satisfying marriage. Adjusting to pregnancy and the promise of parenthood. Fitting into the kin network.
(2) Childbearing	Wife-mother Husband-father Infant daughter or son	Having, adjusting to, and encouraging the development of infants. Establishing a satisfying home for both parents and infant(s).
(3) Preschool-age	Wife-mother Husband-father Daughter-sister Son-brother	Adapting to the critical needs and interests of preschool children in stimulating, growth-promoting ways. Coping with energy depletion and lack of privacy as parents.
(4) School-age	Wife-mother Husband-father Daughter-sister Son-brother	Fitting into the community of school-age families in constructive ways. Encouraging children's educational achievement.
(5) Teenage	Wife-mother Husband-father Daughter-sister Son-brother	Balancing freedom with responsibility as teenagers mature and emancipate themselves. Establishing postparental interests and careers as growing parents.
(6) Launching center	Wife-mother-grandmother Husband-father-grandfather Daughter-sister-aunt Son-brother-uncle	Releasing young adults into work, military service, college, and marriage, with appropriate rituals and assistance. Maintaining a supportive home base.
(7) Middle-aged parents	Wife-mother-grandmother Husband-father-grandfather	Rebuilding the marriage relationship. Maintaining kin ties with older and younger generations.
(8) Aging family members	Widow/widower Wife-mother-grandmother Husband-father-grandfather	Coping with bereavement and living alone. Closing the family home or adapting it to aging. Adjusting to retirement.

SOURCE: Table 85, "Stage-Critical Family Developmental Tasks through the Family Life Cycle" (p. 179) in MARRIAGE AND FAMILY DEVELOPMENT, Fifth Edition by Evelyn Millis Duvall. (J. B. Lippincott) Copyright © 1957, 1967, 1971, 1977 by J. B. Lippincott Company. Reprinted by permission of Harper & Row, Publishers, Inc.

She believes that major problems are caused by events that occur off-time as in the too early or too late birth of a child, or when the death of a parent occurs during childhood.

Carter and McGoldrick (1980) have conceptualized the family life cycle in terms of the multigenerational family system. Broadening the view of a family to include three or more generations is essential, they feel, in order to understand the enormous impact of influences and stresses passing down the generations in the family. Their formulation of family life stages focuses on the major points at which family members enter or exit from the family system, upsetting the family balance (Table 3.2). They see the principal underlying process to be negotiated by families as "the expansion, contraction, and realignment of the relationship system to support the entry, exist, and development of family members in a functional way." Focus is on the shifts in relationships that they deem to be necessary if the family is going to be successful in moving from one life stage to the next.

The worker who needs to understand how a family must shift its attitudes and modify its relationships in adapting to changing life stages will find that Table 3.2 is useful. Again, the first task is to match the family being assessed with its life stage in the column on the left. As an example, for the family with an unattached young adult an emotional process of transition, as listed in the middle column, involves the acceptance on the part of family members that parent-offspring separation is expected to take place. In order to proceed developmentally, as conceptualized in the right column, the following changes are expected to take place for family members: (1) differentiation of self in relation to family of origin, (2) development of intimate peer relationship, and (3) establishment of self in work. Applying this to practice, if the family problems involve a young adult, the task is one of examining how the family is dealing with the process of accepting parent-offspring separation. Further understanding would involve examining whether the problems are related to the expected developmental tasks. Similarly, for the family identified as a newly married couple, the emotional process of transitions to his life stage involves the necessity to make a commitment to a new system. In order to accomplish this, and to proceed developmentally, the couple is expected to: (1) form a marital system and (2) realign relationships with extended families and friends. To apply this to practice, if the couple is experiencing problems at this life stage, the worker would examine the problem in terms of whether or not they are able to negotiate the appropriate emotional process and carry out the tasks that are expected for this life stage.

For families going through divorce, Carter and McGoldrick view the transitional stages of divorce and remarriage as having specific phases. These are characterized by emotional processes of transition and by prerequisite attitudes which are required to deal with the developmental issues appropriate to that phase of family life (Table 3.3).

To identify the phase of the divorce process that a family is experiencing, the worker examines the column on the left. If a family is in the initial phase of this stage, that phase is identified as "the decision to divorce." The worker then sees that in order to deal with the emotional process at this time of transition, the requisite attitude is the "acceptance of the inability to resolve marital tensions," as shown in the middle column. The developmental issues specific to this first phase of the divorce process are the "acceptance of one's own part in the failure of the marriage" as listed in the column on the right. In working with a family in this phase, the worker would focus interventive plans on helping the husband and wife to accomplish these tasks. In each succeeding phase of the divorce process, the chart can be used accordingly as a tool that cléarly delineates what is expectable functioning at this stage in the family life cycle.

Table 3.4 illustrates the steps to be taken in remarried family formation with prerequisite attitudes and developmental issues listed. The first step, in the column on the left, is "entering a new relationship." To accomplish this step, the prerequisite

(Text continued on page 52.)

TABLE 3.2 The Stages of the Family Life Cycle

Family Life Cycle Stage	Emotional Process of Transition: Key Principles	Second-Order Changes in Family Status Required to Proceed Developmentally	
(1) Between Families: The Unattached Young Adult	Accepting parent-offspring separation	(a)	Differentiation of self in relation to family of origin
		(b)	Development of intimate peer relationships
		(c)	Establishment of self in work
(2) The Joining of Families Through Marriage: The Newly Married Couple	Commitment to new system	(a)	Formation of marital system
		(b)	Realignment of relationships with extended families and friends to include spouse
(3) The Family with Young Children	Accepting new members into the system	(a)	Adjusting marital system to make space for child(ren)
		(b)	Taking on parenting roles
		(c)	Realignment of relationships with extended family to include parenting and grandparenting roles
(4) The Family with Adolescents	Increasing flexibility of family boundaries	(a)	Shifting of parent-child relationships to permit adolescent to move in and out of system
		(b)	Refocus on mid-life marital and career issues
		(c)	Beginning shift toward concerns for older generation
(5) Launching Children and Moving On	Accepting a multitude of exits from and entries into the family system	(a)	Renegotiation of marital system as a dyad
		(b)	Development of adult relationships between grown children and parents
		(c)	Realignment of relationships to include in-laws and grandchildren
		(d)	Dealing with disabilities and death of parents (grandparents)
(6) The Family in Later Life	Accepting the shifting of generational roles	(a)	Maintaining own and/or couple functioning and interests in face of physiological decline: exploration of new familial and social role options
		(b)	Support for a more central role for middle generation
		(c)	Making room in the system for the wisdom and experience of the older generation without overfunctioning for them
		(d)	Dealing with loss of spouse, siblings, and other peers, and preparation for own death. Life review and integration.

SOURCE: *The Family Life Cycle* edited by Elizabeth A. Carter and Monica McGoldrick. Copyright 1980 by Gardner Press, Inc., New York. Reprinted by permission of publisher.

TABLE 3.3 Dislocations of the Family Cycle Requiring Additional Steps to Restabilize and Proceed Developmentally

Phase	Emotional Process of Transition Prerequisite Attitude	Developmental Issues
DIVORCE		
(1) The decision to divorce	Accepting of inability to resolve marital tensions	Acceptance of one's own part in the failure of the marriage
(2) Planning the break up of the system	Supporting viable arrangements for all parts of the system	(a) Working cooperatively on problems of custody, visitation, finances (b) Dealing with extended family about the divorce
(3) Separation	(A) Willingness to continue co-operative coparental relationship (B) Work on resolution of attachment to spouse	(a) Mourning loss of intact family (b) Restructuring marital and parent-child relationships; adaptation to living apart (c) Realignment of relationships with extended family; staying connected with spouse's extended family
(4) The divorce	More work on emotional divorce: Overcoming hurt, anger, guilt	(a) Mourning loss of intact family: giving up fantasies of reunion (b) Retrieval of hopes, dreams, expectations from the marriage (c) Staying connected with extended families
POST-DIVORCE FAMILY		
(1) Single-parent family	Willingness to maintain parental contact with ex-spouse and support contact of children with ex-spouse and his or her family	(a) Making flexible visitation arrangements with ex-spouse and his or her family (b) Rebuilding own social network
(2) Single-parent (Noncustodial)	Willingness to maintain parental contact with ex-spouse and support custodial parent's relationship with children	(a) Finding ways to continue effective parenting relationships with children

SOURCE: *The Family Life Cycle* edited by Elizabeth A. Carter and Monica McGoldrick. Copyright 1980 by Gardner Press, Inc., New York. Reprinted by permission of the publisher.

TABLE 3.4 Remarried Family Formation: A Developmental Outline

Steps	Prerequisite Attitude	Developmental Issues
(1) Entering the new relationship	Recovery from loss of first marriage (adequate "emotional divorce")	Recommitment to marriage and to forming a family with readiness to deal with the complexity and ambiguity
(2) Conceptualizing and planning new marriage and family	Accepting one's own fears and those of new spouse and children about remarriage and forming a stepfamily	(a) Work on openness in the new relationships to avoid pseudomutuality.
	Accepting need for time and patience for adjustment to complexity and ambiguity of (A) Multiple new roles (B) Boundaries: space, time, membership, and authority. (C) Affective Issues: guilt, loyalty conflicts, desire for mutuality, unresolvable past hurts	(b) Plan for maintenance of cooperative coparental relationships with ex-spouses (c) Plan to help children deal with fears, loyalty conflicts, and membership in two systems. (d) Realignment of relationships with extended family to include new spouse and children. (e) Plan maintenance of connections for children with extended family of ex-spouse(s).
(3) Remarriage and reconstitution of family	Final resolution of attachment to previous spouse and ideal of "intact" family;	(a) Restructuring family boundaries to allow for inclusion of new spouse—stepparent.
	Acceptance of a different model of family with permeable boundaries	(b) Realignment of relationships throughout subsystems to permit interweaving of several systems. (c) Making room for relationships of all children with biological (noncustodial) parents, grandparents, and other extended family. (d) Sharing memories and histories to enhance step-family integration.

SOURCE: *The Family Life Cycle* edited by Elizabeth A. Carter and Monica McGoldrick. Copyright 1980 by Gardner Press, Inc., N.Y. Reprinted by permission of the publisher.

attitude listed in the middle column is "recovery from loss of first marriage (adequate 'emotional divorce')." Adopting this attitude is seen as enabling the persons to deal with the developmental issues concerned with "recommitment to marriage and to forming a family with readiness to deal with the complexity and ambiguity" of the new relationship. The developmental issues appropriate to steps in the formation of the remarried family are shown in the column on the right. The worker who uses this chart will have guidelines available for planning interventions aimed at supporting development of the family in this life stage.

The formulations of the family life cycle discussed in this section are of considerable value to the worker who is in the process of assessing a family where neglect or abuse is the problem. Using the tables for identifying the family's stage in the life cycle provides a framework for understanding what the developmental tasks are for the family as a whole and for its members individually. If, for example, a family with an adolescent is unable to grant an appropriate degree of independence to their child, serious problems are likely to develop.

> When Michael, 16, the oldest of four children was treated in an emergency room for a bruised eye, it was learned that he and his father had had a confrontation, which led to the father's punching him. In a family interview with the hospital social worker, the father acknowledged his loss of control and burst into tears. He told of his frustration and disappointment with himself for not being the kind of parent to Michael that his father was to him. He explained that his strict but loving father imposed rigid restrictions and did not permit him to go out with girls until he was 18. Since he accepted this prohibition, he could not understand why Michael would not do as he had done but instead sneaked out to go to a party with a girl from his class. Michael's mother agreed that her husband's rules should have been obeyed.

Understanding that this was the first time that this family had faced problems such as this was important for the worker because many families make a commitment to change as a result of experiences and becomes better able to cope with life stage stresses. Families are dynamic and are always capable of change. When a pattern is repetitive in a family, however, it is viewed as more serious. Although community standards are violated when any abuse takes place, making a moral judgment that an abusive parent is "bad" may reflect failure on the part of the worker to understand that the family has not yet negotiated the process of accepting the requirements of that life stage. It can be seen that as the needs of a family change, family norms are expected to change. Behavior that is expected or accepted at one life stage may be substantially different from what is expected or accepted at another life stage. Consequently, evaluating the synchronization between the expectations of that life stage and the adjustment which the family has made is a vital step in the assessment process.

Theoreticians concerned with the relationship between family life stage and appropriate developmental tasks have noticed that it is more likely for problems to develop when the family has been through a change in life stage and when a major life event has taken place, that is, addition or loss of a family member (Hadley et al., 1974). Difficulties in adjusting to the behaviors in a new life stage are conspicuous in families that have avoided resolution of early tasks. Such families are likely to demonstrate chronic difficulties in family interaction (Solomon, 1973). Some families have particular problems in adapting to a new stage in the family life cycle. Haley (1973) believes that focusing on predictable life stages calls attention to the individual or family who do not meet the socially expectable goals and therefore may be perceived as different. Consequently, it is important to note that significant deviation from the norm may serve as an indication that an impending or present problem can be expected. It is not uncommon for maltreated children to be those whose birth was unplanned and came about at a time when their parents were unready to cope with the responsibilities of parenthood. Children born out of wedlock or to teenaged mothers are at risk due to difficulties faced by the parents in accommodating to an unaccustomed life stage and to tasks for which they were unprepared.

Theory related to the family life cycle has largely focused on intact and reconstituted families, but it must also take into account those families in which there is, for an extended period of time, only one parent. Recent demographic data reveal a sizeable increase in single-parent families principally as the result of divorce. According to data collected in March 1980, the Census Bureau reports that one of every five children for a total of 12.2 million, up 4 million from 1970, lived with one parent (New York Times, October 18, 1981). Those children who lived in a single-parent home with only their mother were 91.5% of the total and the remaining 8.5% lived with their father. Of those children who lived with their mothers, 67% lived with a mother who was either divorced or separated, 14.1% lived with mothers who were never married, and 10.4% lived with widowed mothers (U.S. Bureau of the Census, 1981). For whites and blacks the picture is different. Three times as many black children as white children were living with only one parent (44% versus 14%).

Practitioners who understand the impact of these phenomena on family functioning recognize that both parents and children are substantially affected by living in a single-parent household. Such families are generally affected by increased economic hardships; task overload, which may be reflected in family disorganization; social isolation; and dysfunctional parent-child relationships (Beal, 1980). It is worth nothing that the cause of the disruption in the family life cycle, whether it is either divorce or death, significantly influences the nature of the resulting impact. Widowed mothers are more likely to have the support of their husbands' extended family and members of the community than are divorced mothers. They tend to feel higher self-esteem and are less likely to be self-blaming for their situation compared with their divorced counterparts.

The stage of the family life cycle is another influence that has been shown to affect how a family adjusts to change in status. In a family without children, divorce or widowhood has fewer immediate consequences. The greatest stress is usually found in families with young children. Children under 5 seem to have greater difficulty in adjusting to parental divorce than children over 5 (Wallerstein and Kelly, 1980). Latency age and adolescent children generally experience fewer developmental deviations than do younger children but have been shown to be affected in their social and academic functioning. It has been observed that if children are the focus of parental projections, they are more likely to respond with affective and behavioral reactions to divorce. Adolescents have the advantage of maintaining contact with extended family and in influencing custody decisions. However, they frequently are thrust into inappropriate roles by dependent parents.

Understanding how single-parent families differ from intact families is critical for assessment. Evaluations of families must be objective in the light of information that has been gathered to avoid the tendency to stereotype. Single-parent families of all types tend to be negatively viewed by school personnel, according to a survey conducted by a parents' right group (New York Times, February 2, 1981). This survey of 1200 single parents revealed that children with one parent in the home are negatively stereotyped. Homes designated as "broken" are perceived pejoratively and children's problems are attributed as related to their parents' single status whether or not this is the case.

It is important that workers not stereotype families or adopt judgmental attitudes. Rather, it is necessary to recognize that there are different roles and tasks in single-parent families and adjustments are necessary to cope with these roles (Table 3.3). From the ecological viewpoint, support systems such as grandparents, surrogate caretakers, and the broad range of community resources must be mobilized, where needed, to enable single-parent families to function at the highest possible level.

Throughout the assessment process, focus on the family life cycle enhances the worker's understanding of the stresses that impinge on the family. Therefore, before interventions are planned, it is always necessary to evaluate the family's life stage; the tasks it can be expected to carry out; and, finally, the assessment of how they are, in fact, carried out. Only then can it be clearly understood whether this is a family undergoing the normal stresses of its life stage or whether it is a family that is characteristically dysfunctional as it experiences each life stage.

Family Life Cycle Exercises

(1) This exercise is helpful in relating the concepts of the family life cycle to work with families. It links a family's life stage to those tasks that are necessary for the family to carry out in order to meet the needs of its members. It is a means of assessing whether the functioning of the family fulfills the expectations of society.

   (a) Select a client family and match it with its life stage as shown in Table 3.1. Choose one of the developmental tasks from the column on the right and evaluate whether the family is carrying out this stage-appropriate task. Continue to assess the family and its members in relation to each of the tasks that is critical to its life stage.

   (b) What interventions would be useful in helping this family to meet the needs of its members?

(2) This exercise provides practice in linking the life stage tasks to the processes and attitudes that are required for appropriate family functioning at the various stages in the family life cycle.

   (a) Select a family you know well. Match the family with its family cycle life stage as shown in Table 3.2.

(b) Examine the process of transition for this family's life stage. Next, consider the changes in family status required to proceed developmentally. Compare what you know about this family's adaptation to its life stage and note whether it is adapting to meet its family members' needs. If not, think about what interventions could be used to promote the appropriate development of the family.

(c) Carry out the same exercise with Tables 3.3 and 3.4 selecting families whose status matches the one in the table.

(d) For additional practice, choose families from each of the life stages and carry out the exercise accordingly.

(e) Can you identify families with whom you have worked where knowledge of the family life cycle and its stage-appropriate task would have changed your assessment? Your interventions?

Summary

The framework for the assessment of a family includes an understanding of the problem, the family as a system, the environment of the family, and the family life cycle.

(1) The client's problem is best viewed in terms of its origin, duration, urgency, the agency response, and the family response.

(2) The family is understood to be a system consisting of individuals who are related to each other in a more or less stable way. Its tasks are carried out by subgroups that can be formed by generation, sex, interests, abilities, or by function. The behavior of any family member affects all of the other family members and, consequently, the overall balance of the family.

All families have boundaries that may be either open, partly open, or closed. The permeability of the boundary determines how available the family is to new people and new ideas.

Unusually close or distant family relationships tend to promote dysfunction within the family system. Blurred boundaries of the subsystem reflecting lack of differentiation may result in enmeshment, while the other extreme, overly rigid boundaries reflecting isolation and unavailability of family members, may result in disengagement.

Communication patterns, both verbal and nonverbal, convey significant information about the family. Attitudes and values are revealed by interactions between family members in terms of who communicates with whom about which topics. Unclear communications and conflicting double bind messages are believed to be important factors in the development of many serious family problems.

The family structure consists of the various roles that are enacted within the family with traditional role performances expected to meet family needs. Problems may result if roles are ambiguous, conflicting, inflexible; if there is a lack congruence; or if the family is unattuned to the prevailing cultural norms. Roles may be either ascribed or assumed reflecting formal or informal socioemotional functions.

(3) The total environment of the family must be considered in assessing its ability to meet significant needs. This ecological view stresses both the physical environment as well as the social environment. Assessing gaps in services and establishing linkages between families and available resources are essential tasks for all human service workers.

(4) Knowledge of the family life cycle facilitiates the assessment of a family's life stage. This knowledge enhances the worker's ability to identify predictable life stresses and to recognize whether family norms and behaviors are appropriate to that life stage. It is important to assess single-parent families with an understanding of how this phenomenon affects the roles and tasks of the various life stages.

Chapter 4

METHODS OF ASSESSMENT

Making an assessment of a family is a demanding task in any setting and requires a high degree of knowledge and skill. Knowledge of theoretical concepts related to an understanding of the family, discussed in the previous chapter, provides the basis for a focused assessment. The skills needed by the worker are discussed in this chapter.

There are three principal approaches that have been used effectively in assessing families: (1) the interview, (2) direct observation, and (3) the use of checklists or inventories.

(1) The interview is a face-to-face meeting between the worker and one or more family members for the mutual purpose of helping and gathering information. It may be initiated by either the worker or a family member with the setting and length variable, and it may be the sole contact or one of a series of contacts. Dynamic family system-focused tools, for example, the ecomap, the genogram, and family sculpture, are especially useful in family interviews and are discussed below.

(2) Direct observation for assessment purposes is focused on family members individually and how they interact as a family group. Observation is made of the family in the office and sometimes in the home environment. It may be structured or unstructured, with the worker as an uninvolved observer, as a

participant observer, or as a leader-and-initiator observer (Compton and Galaway, 1979).

(3) The checklist or inventory is a guide to the factors that are deemed to be essential to the functioning of a family, and include environmental, physical, social, and emotional factors. Taken together, the factors provide an overview of the family and are a means for rating their strengths and limitations. These methods are not mutually exclusive, but rather each offer a special focus and contribution toward evaluating the capacity of a family to meet the needs of its members. In the following pages, we will explore a number of tools that can be used in the family interview process. Direct observation and inventories will be discussed in chapter 5.

The Interview

The interview involves the parents or their surrogates and, where appropriate, the children, as well. In some instances, the interview may also involve members of the extended family and other people who have knowledge of the family, for example, teachers, neighbors, ministers. However, prior to meeting with family members, it is essential to review all of the facts about the family that are available in the agency records, including referral information.

In the interview, useful information can generally be elicited by asking both direct and indirect questions, encouraging comments, paraphrasing, reflecting feelings, and summarizing. Listening and observing are essential elements and are implicit in every phase of interviewing (Schubert, 1971).

It is important to create a comfortable climate in order to enhance the receptivity of the children and the parents to the interview and to encourage their participation and cooperation. An atmosphere of openness suggests that the worker is inviting the family members and others to share in the assessment process. Throughout the interview, its purpose must be clearly in focus so that the importance of the goal to be accomplished is communicated. This will help to ensure that the responsibility for collecting the necessary information is understood.

The goal of the interview is a significant factor in terms of how the interview is conducted. If circumstances require that a vital decision be made quickly, the interview must be structured so that within the framework of the allotted time, all of the necessary information is obtained. If, as is more usual, circumstances permit a fuller assessment before intervention plans must be made, then the interview can be used in conjunction with other assessment tools, and there may be more flexibility in its structure.

Let us go back to our earlier discussion of child neglect and abuse. You will see implications for your own practice. Whenever there is a strong suspicion of serious neglect or child abuse, a special technique known as investigative interviewing is necessary (Sgroi, 1982). The contribution of the family to the abuse must be assessed, with the strengths and weaknesses of every family member identified. It is important to learn whether the child's victimization was a one-time-only event or was part of a pattern of less serious abuses. Determination of whether the abuse was a reaction to unusual circumstances is called for as part of the assessment. Sensitive and focused investigative interviewing with specific questions will make it possible to obtain the required information to establish the facts needed to protect the child. In cases where legal intervention may be necessary, workers must collect explicit data to substantiate allegations of abuse.

Another method of interviewing utilizes dynamic family-system-focused assessment tools. While these can take many different forms, three of the most widely used are the ecomap, the genogram, and family sculpture. Although these three methods have different origins, they have been grouped together for assessment purposes by Ann Hartman in *Finding Families* (1979). These tools are especially helpful in encouraging active collaboration between family members and the worker in collecting subjective as well as objective data. The ecomap, as discussed earlier, provides a structure for diagramming the connections between a family system and the other systems in their ecological field. The genogram involves the family tree, which includes significant people and events over several generations. Family sculpture is a means by which family members create a live family protrait. All of these tools will be discussed in greater detail.

When working with nonverbal family members, these collaborative approaches are of particular value. Active involvement in the interview tends to stimulate participation by family members who might otherwise be reticent and withholding. It has been demonstrated that use of dynamic stimuli such as the ecomap, genogram, or family sculpture engages the client as a cooperating member of a problem-solving team whose goal it is to collect valid information, assess capacity for change, and to bring about change in functioning. These methods have become recognized for their usefulness in assessment since, in addition to gathering factual information, they enable the worker to learn about personal reactions and the meanings that are attributed to family events and processes. These assessment tools may be used differentially depending upon the client and the situation in the interview. As each of them is discussed in detail, the indications for their use become clear.

Ecomap

To understand the various factors contributing to a situation of child neglect or abuse, it is necessary to assess the balance between a family and the resources in its environment. Polansky et al. (1979) have found that neglectful families are not in helping networks to the same extent as other families of similar social position. Constructing the ecomap is a dynamic way of diagramming the connections between a family and the people and institutions in its life space. This assessment tool was developed in 1975 by Ann Hartman to help public child welfare workers examine the needs of families.

The ecomap provides a visual overview of the complex ecological system of the family and shows its organizational patterns and relationships. It maps the major systems that are part of the family's environment and provide a picture of the balance between the demands and resources of the family system. In highlighting the nature of the connections between the family and its ecological system, the ecomap demonstrates the flow of resources from the environment to the family as well as deprivations and unmet needs (Hartman, 1978).

As the ecomap is developed with the involvement of family members, it provides the worker and the family with an understanding of the stresses on the family system as well as the available supports, and family members are likely to feel more comfortable and less defensive about providing information (Hartman, 1979). Using a structured map simplifies the procedure for the worker and clarifies for the participating family members how the various systems in their ecological field relate to their family.

Figure 4.1 shows the structure used to construct an ecomap. Some of the circles are labeled to identify typical systems in a family's environment. In the large circle in the center of the diagram, the family can be pictured by using symbols that represent family members and their relationships. Squares will be added to depict males and small circles added to depict females; they will be joined together forming a family tree to portray relationships. Connections are drawn onto the map to show relationships between the family and the systems in its environment, with significant people identified for the systems. Note that the unlabeled circles provide the opportunity for the participating family to suggest additional people or institutions with which it has relationships. In this way, the ecomap becomes individualized for the family in the interview.

As an illustration of how the ecomap is used, the case of Gloria and her family is discussed below, followed by the presentation of a complete ecomap that portrays this family and its relationship to the systems in its environment (Figure 4.2).

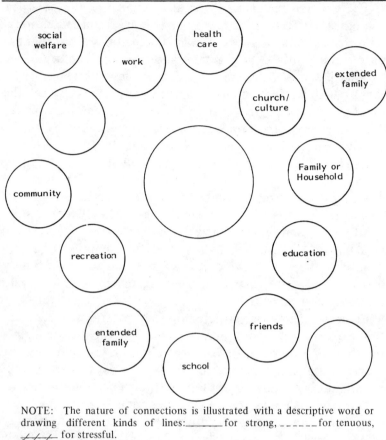

NOTE: The nature of connections is illustrated with a descriptive word or drawing different kinds of lines:_____ for strong, _ _ _ _ _ _ for tenuous, ⁻/⁻/⁻/⁻ for stressful.
Arrows are drawn along lines to signify flow of energy, or resources:

Figure 4.1: Ecomap

Prior to the interview with Gloria, this referral information was known to the worker:

Gloria is the mother of a 14-year-old girl, Ginger, whom she had voluntarily placed in foster care at birth. Gloria was 15 and in a detention home at the time of Ginger's birth. Gloria's parents maintained little contact with her and showed no interest in her child. Ginger has lived all her years with an elderly couple, the

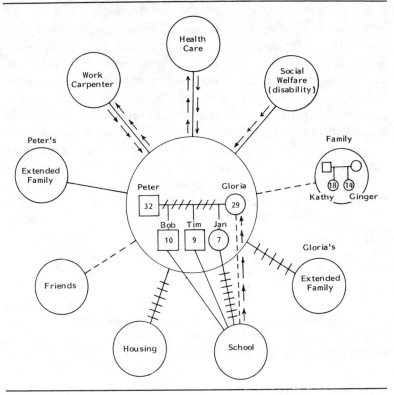

Figure 4.2

P.s, who are religious and have strict moral standards. They have one daughter, Kathy, 18, who usually conforms to her parents' standards. Since age 12, Ginger has developed school problems and her foster parents have been increasingly upset with her interest in boys, loud music, and dancing.

Gloria kept in contact with Ginger until she was 4, but has not been in touch for the past ten years since she married Peter and had three children in quick succession. Two years ago Peter left her and the children but returns occasionally. At present he is not living at home. Recently, Ginger learned of her mother's whereabouts and began visiting her. Now she has asked Gloria if she can join her family.

In the interview with Gloria, more information was elicited by the worker, principally as a result of working together with her on the ecomap. It can be seen in Figure 4.2 that Gloria's family is pictured in the large circle with the stressful relationship between Gloria and Peter indicated by the crossed line. Peter was described as a carpenter who likes his work and earns good wages when construction jobs are available, and this is shown on the ecomap by positive connections between Peter and his work. Gloria complained, however, that his irregular support does not provide enough income to afford better housing and she was very dejected as she described how their apartment had deteriorated. Not that their connection to housing is depicted as stressful.

Gloria explained that she is unable to work because of a chronic kidney condition that requires treatment at a local hospital. She keeps her appointments regularly and said that the hospital has provided good care for her and her family. She also acknowledged that the small disability payment she receives has made it possible to her to buy some necessities for the children. This information was translated onto the ecomap into positive connections with both the health care and social welfare systems.

Problems continue to exist between Gloria and her extended family. She contrasts this with the relationship between Peter and his family, which is a close one. She often feels alone with her problems since she has always had difficulty in keeping friends. As the worker filled in the various connections, Gloria remarked that it was good to have someone to tell about her situation and how she feels.

When Gloria discussed her children, it became clear that while her sons Bob and Tim were doing well in school Jan, her daughter, was experiencing adjustment problems. Although the school social worker had contacted her, Gloria has not followed through in meeting with her because she felt it would remind her of her own problems when she was her daughter's age. These comments were noted and diagrammed accordingly. After the ecomap was completed, Gloria was very much involved in studying this visual description of her family and its relationship to the people and institutions in the environment. She expressed satisfaction that the worker had "gotten everything right."

This case illustration demonstrates how the process of ecomapping encourages collaboration between the worker and the client in collecting information. Engaging in this joint activity provided an opportunity for Gloria and the worker to begin developing a relationship based upon mutual concerns and trust.

Participation in the process of ecomapping and studying the finished diagram enhances discussions that follow in terms of planning how a family can draw upon resources that it requires for improved functioning. This approach often provides entry into a closed family system for establishing linkages to underused resources. It may also reveal a need for services that do not exist and that can become a focus for further planning.

Human service workers in a wide variety of settings will find the ecomap to be an easy and effective means of learning about a family's connections with the systems in its environment. It is especially recommended for use with clients who have difficulty in sharing information either because they tend to be nonverbal or because they feel threatened by a request to reveal information about themselves. It is not unusual to find clients to be fearful of negative consequences if they tell about themselves. The process of ecomapping allows for initial questions to be phrased in broad, general terms that do not seem overly intrusive. "Do you have much family?" Do you work at a job?" "Are people helpful in your neighborhood?" Gradually, more specific questions may be asked such as: "Are you close to your family?" "How do you like your work?" "Are there neighbors you can call upon for help in this situation?"

Ecomap Exercise

You will find that constructing an ecomap of your own family is a worthwhile exercise as a means of gaining familiarity with the method. Examining the family for an ecological perspective is, for most workers, a new and stimulating experience. It provides an opportunity to sensitize yourself to the role of the client and the knowledge gained of your family is always meaningful. Ecomapping can be carried out by yourself but it is preferable to do it in conjunction with a colleague or supervisor. Alternately role playing the part of the worker and the client in a simulated interview will maximize this learning experience.

When this exercise has been practiced and you have a sound grasp of the technique, it is important to begin using it in assessment interviews with family members. At the end of an interview, it is helpful to analyze the value of this tool in terms of data collected, data needed, and advantages and disadvantages of the method. For this purpose, the Evaluation of Assessment Method form is available at the end of the next chapter. Use this as a model and make some additional copies for your repeated use. When you have evaluated this method and also those that follow in this chapter, including genogram and family sculpture, the use of one or more of these methods deemed appropriate for a particular family will contribute significantly to the assessment process.

Genogram

The ecomap is used as an adjunct for interviewing focused on the relationship between the family system and its environment. By contrast, the genogram is a valuable assessment tool for learning about a family's history over a period of time.

Based upon the concept of a family tree, it usually includes data about three or more generations of the family, which provides a longitudinal perspective. As a diagram of the family's relationship system, the genogram provides a graphic picture of family geneology, including significant life events (birth, marriage, separation, divorce, illness, death); identification (racial, social class, ethnic, religious); occupations; places of family residence. Family patterns emerge, providing vital information that frequently relates to behavior contributing to the family's problems.

The process of diagramming this visual interpretation of the family in the course of an interview offers a unique opportunity for family members and the worker and enables the family to see itself as a unit. The genogram is a structure for the sharing of information; at the same time, it encourages the expression of feelings about the people and events that are discussed. Constructing a genogram may begin in an initial interview with the use of a prepared genogram outline showing the family that this is a usual procedure in this setting. Even reticent family members are generally willing to share abundant information and are often surprised to recognize that while they know much about some areas of family history, they know little about other areas. As information is discussed, it often becomes clear that spouses or children are unfamiliar with information that it was assumed they knew. Reluctance to share information must be respected by the worker, as it may be indicative of family history that is distressing or embarrassing. It is not unusual to find that information that was previously withheld may be revealed at a later time as trust in the worker develops.

The following case illustration demonstrates how the genogram was used as an assessment tool by a hospital social worker who was called to the emergency room to investigate suspected child abuse. It shows how this nonthreatening approach was used to learn about a family's background.

Ann, 2, was brought by her mother to the emergency room of the hospital for treatment of a broken arm. When she was examined, welts were found on her back and the question of possible child abuse was raised. The hospital social worker asked Ann's parents, Jean and Bert, to meet with him. After a brief initial interview, they agreed to return for another interview.

The social worker was very supportive in discussing how parents sometimes can be very upset when a child is uncooperative. Jean agreed that sometimes she felt overwhelmed with pressures and may have lost control of her anger when Ann disobeyed her. The social worker suggested that the construction of a genogram was a useful way for parents to learn about why their family is having problems. Together Bert and Jean provided information about the family (Figure 4.3).

The process of drawing a genogram encouraged Jean to describe her life situation. She told of the estrangement from her parents and sister since the time of her marriage at 17 to Jim, her first husband, in 1959. The marriage was unacceptable to her parents so that when it ended—shortly after her son Steve was born, as her parents had predicted it would—Jean felt too embarrassed to call them. She married Bert soon after and had two more children in a short space of time. As she gave information, the social worker began drawing the genogram. Jean and her parents, Joe and Mary; her sister, Sally; and her first husband's family were entered on it. While their names, ages, and occupations were filled in, Jean became noticeably involved in sharing the data.

Jean said that after she and Jim had separated, he finished college, became a teacher, and married Betty in 1963. Jim and Betty moved to California to be near Betty's family, but Jim kept in touch with his son Steve. Jim and Betty had twins, a son and daughter, and Jean said they seemed to have a warm family life. When Steve graduated high school, he asked his father if he could live with him and Betty in California and attend college there. They sent him a plane ticket and he moved away. He wrote to his mother and her family occasionally, but seemed to prefer his new life with his father's family. As Jean told of this, she became tearful.

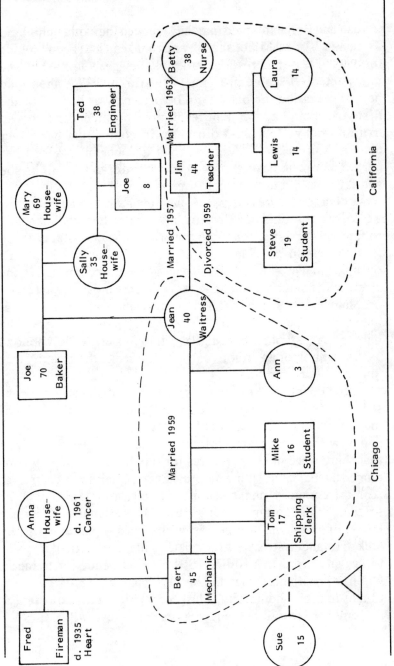

Figure 4.3

71

Jean and Bert explained that they enjoyed their other children, Tom, age 20, and Mike, age 18, and that Jean had been looking forward to lessened responsibility as they grew up. When she unexpectedly became pregnant with Ann in 1977, she found herself resenting the baby even before she was born. For the first year, Ann had frequent respiratory problems and was an irritable baby. Jean had difficulty in controlling her anger toward Ann as the child grew older and began to assert her negativism. The past year seemed most difficult of all as she and Ann battled until Jean lost control.

Adding to the pressures, the past few months had been particularly stressful since Bert lost his job and had not been able to find another one. Jean found work as a waitress at night so that she could provide some income. At this point, Jean's occupation was entered on the genogram as she pointed to the circle with her name. Then they said that the most recent family problem was learning that Tom's girlfriend had become pregnant four months ago. Tom agree to help pay the costs of the baby's birth out of his earnings as a shipping clerk. Bert nodded as the symbol for an unborn baby was added to their family tree joined to Tom and Sue.

At the conclusion of the interview, with the genogram constructed, the social worker reassured the parents that he did, indeed, understand the difficulty that they were experiencing in coping with so many stressful areas in their lives. He recognized that there were many pressures for this family with an unemployed husband, including the pregnancy of their son's girlfriend, Ann's frequently negativistic behavior, and Jean's lack of someone close to turn to for support. Her alienation from her family of origin and the contrast with what she perceived as the lack of financial stresses in her sister's life lent particular strain to her situation. In addition, Steve's preference for living in California with his father and his family appeared to be a rejection of Jean and her family. The geographic separation made it difficult for Jean to feel encouraged that Steve will return for visits on a regular basis. Also, the factual data supplied about Jim's family, in terms of his and Betty's career attainments, raise the likelihood that Jean may feel resentful of her former husband's stable economic status while she is struggling.

The knowledge gained in the course of filling in the genogram suggested to the social worker that there were a number of possible interventions that they could consider as appropriate in alleviating the pressures on the family and in preventing child abuse. By participating in the assessment process, Jean and Bert were involved in seeking solutions to their problems.

The case illustration shows how a multigenerational view of the family provides data that are useful in learning about family members, their relationships and roles, family themes and patterns, and nodal events. This information provides the worker with a basis for planning interventions. In this case, the explicit information provided by the parents, Jean and Bert, contributes significantly to understanding the dynamics that influenced their loss of control and the resultant abuse of their child. However, implicit in the family situation are other factors that may bear upon the behavior of the parents. They are worth examining as they help to explain how the family members function and why this family has particularly difficult problems in coping with stress. Examples of such information that a worker may regard as pertinent to assessment are the following:

(1) events that were off-time in the family life cycle, for example, an early marriage, a late birth, an unplanned teenaged pregnancy;

(2) cut-offs in two generations, first from the extended family, and then by a son;

(3) the victimization of an only daughter among four children, raising questions about the child's role in the life of the mother;

(4) the question of whether a marriage very soon after a divorce contributed to it or was a reaction to it.

Genogram Exercise

You will find that drawing a genogram of your family is a stimulating exercise. As in the case of the ecomap, you may undertake it by yourself or you may carry it out in a role-playing situation with a colleague enacting the role of the worker. If you find gaps in your knowledge of your family, make an effort to fill them in so that this becomes a valid learning experience. When you have added as much information as you can and you consider the genogram complete, stop and think about it. How did it feel to be tracing your family's history? Did you learn anything new or unexpected about your family? Did you see trends or patterns with which you were previously unfamiliar? Did you recall any events that were uncomfortable and usually suppressed? Did you find connections that provoked new assessments of relationships in your family?

Reinforcement of the learning that has taken place can be accomplished by teaching colleagues or supervisees to do genograms. In addition to deriving benefit from the practice itself, it will be worthwhile to carry on discussions with others who are involved in using this assessment tool so that you can provide feedback for each other about the experience. Begin using the genogram in your work with families but, as with all assessment tools, use it selectively. Decide, first, whether the family members are ready to examine their family history. If a family is in a state of crisis, they may not be prepared to focus on anything but how to resolve the crisis situation as quickly as possible. When you have used the genogram, remember to evaluate its efficacy by employing the Evaluation of Assessment Method form at the end of the next chapter for this purpose.

Family Sculpture

Family interviewing can be further enriched through the use of family sculpture to assess family relationships and interactions. Growing out of the family therapy movement, this is a tool that engages the family in a dynamic process whereby they create a live family portrait. It is particularly effective with nonverbal clients as a means of portraying the family relationship system. In the interview, the worker explains to the family that this is a useful way to find out what it is like to be in this family. Sometimes it is easier to act out what happens in a family than it is to tell about it. Everyone in the family can show his or her own version of what the family is like by constructing a sculpture.

Each family member has a turn at arranging the other members of the family (or other people substituting for them), one at a time, in the family life space so that the postures and spatial relationships represent actions and feelings (Papp et al., 1973). The sculptor is encouraged to treat each person as if he or she is malleable and made of clay in moving the physical parts of the body to reflect the spatial arrangements, physical actions, and emotional proximity of the family members. The sculptor places each person in a position that characterizes him or her nonverbally. As each person is added to the sculpture, the sculptor gives directions as to positioning until he or she is satisfied that the sculpture reflects his or her picture of the family relationship system.

It is important for family members to permit the sculptor to create the portrait according to his or her own interpretation, with the clear understanding that other members can sculpt their own interpretations when it is their turn.

The G. family was referred to the Youth Services Agency after Carlos, 11, who is physically handicapped, confided to his teacher that sometimes he feels like killing himself. Mr. and

Mrs. G. and their other two children, Pedro, 14, and Carmen, 10, could not seem to explain why Carlos would be unhappy since he did well in school. Carlos kept scowling and repeating, "I don't know why" when asked why he felt so angry and full of despair.

For this uncommunicative family, sculpting their views of the family provided a means for expressing themselves. As each family member took a turn at positioning the other family members (with the worker standing in for the one who was sculpting), family relationships were graphically portrayed.

It became clear that Pedro and Carmen had a close relationship with each other since they were repeatedly positioned next to each other in one pose or another. The parents were shown as distant from their children and each other. Mr. G was either shown at the door leaving or sitting alone and watching TV. Mrs. G. was also portrayed as standing apart from the other family members but was shown facing toward Pedro and Carmen. In each of the sculptures, including his own, Carlos was shown by himself and at a distance from the other family members.

The sculptures illustrated that the G. family saw Carlos as isolated. It demonstrated that the sibling system had excluded him and that the mother, who was seen as distant from all of her children and her husband, showed some connection with Pedro and Carmen but not with Carlos. The father appeared detached from the entire family but seemed to have contacts outside of the home. It was through family sculpture that the family came to the recognition that Carlos also perceived himself as isolated from the rest of the family. This provided the beginning of an explanation for his suicidal feelings. The family and the worker now had important information for planning interventions that would deal with Carlos's isolation and feelings of rejection.

As this case vignette demonstrates, family sculpture is a powerful means of transmitting data such as feelings, attitudes, moods, spatial relationships, and activities. Like pantomime, it is very expressive although in family sculpture there is no movement. This technique is particularly effective in families where there are young children as it involves them in the interview and encourages them to share their feelings. In general, resistant family members are more likely to engage in family sculpture if they feel comfortable with the worker.

Family Sculpture Exercise

In order to practice using family sculpture, it is necessary to have at least as many participants in the sculpting session as there are members of the family to be sculpted. Colleagues and supervisees may be enlisted to join in the exercise as a means of enhancing their assessment skills. Practice may be carried out with simulated families if colleagues are not comfortable using their own families. Some description of the family system and their problems, prior to the sculpting, clarifies who is being protrayed. It is helpful to visualize the family at a particular time and place such as at home on Sunday afternoon. The sculptor is encouraged to be creative in translating perceptions of the family members into physical positions. When the sculptor is satisfied that the portrait is complete and participants and observers have had an opportunity to study it, the participants are asked to step out of their roles and share how they felt physically and emotionally as members of the family. It is worthwhile to discuss how the perceptions about the family contribute to the assessment process and further, how they can be used in planning inverventions.

To use family sculpture with families in your caseload, select carefully those families who are likely to feel comfortable using this method. Offer to demonstrate the technique by using yourself. Show some examples of how emotions or actions are conveyed, for example, anger, concern, affection. This tends to help family members feel more relaxed and willing to participate. At the conclusion of the family sculpture interview, evaluate the method using the form at the end of Chapter 5.

Chapter 5

OBSERVATION AND CHECKLISTS

In adopting an ecological approach to family assessment, the role of observation must be emphasized. In order to become knowledgeable about how a family functions, it is necessary for you to cultivate the art of observation. Critical viewing of how family members interact with other human systems and with the physical and social environment provides useful under-standings of the family's strengths and limitations. Discussion of how checklists and inventories enhance the observation process takes place later in the chapter.

Observation

Observation is a very valuable technique for collecting data. It provides an opportunity to gain perspectives about many aspects of how the family structure operates. Family members' descriptions of their functioning in terms of how roles are performed and how relationships carried out are certainly worthwhile, but must always be interpreted with caution. Such descriptions are likely to reflect beliefs that serve the needs of the family by maintaining the current balance. Some family members do not possess the vocabulary to convey information or may not have the insights to describe family interactions and role performances. Consequently, there is no substitute for direct observation of family dynamics to clarify and validate family members' reports (Tomm and Leahey, 1980).

A skillful observer will capture a great many useful impressions by unobtrusive observation. It is possible to learn how subsystems function and how the family's boundaries operate. If the family is an open or closed system or if it is semipermeable can be assessed by observation. Whether the family is enmeshed or disengaged is discernible by observing the nature of the involvement of family members with each other. Also, how roles are performed may be seen by an astute observer. Are there observable alliances or coalitions? Do parents sit together or apart? Is one child the object of excessive attention on the part of a parent? Does a child act as caretaker while the parents inappropriately distance themselves? The mood of the family may be observed. Is it a calm, reflective family, or is it boisterous, agitated, or lethargic?

The worker's choice of observational techniques affects the quality and accuracy of the information that is gathered. The type of information that is sought determines whether a natural or structured interview is preferable, or whether to use impressionistic or formalized procedures and to act as a participant or nonparticipant observer (Pincus and Minahan 1973). In general, practitioners carry out their obserservations in natural situations whenever they are in direct contact with clients. When specific information is sought, a structured observation may take place.

At a Senior Citizens Center, an aged grandmother confided her fears to the community worker that her grandson Eddie, 8, threatened that one day he will "get even" and might set fire to their house. She explained that her daughter, Mrs. R., who was deserted by her husband, continually singles Eddie out for harsh ciriticism while she is more more tolerant of her daughers Patty, 9, and Laura, 7.

An outreach worker contacted Mrs. R. and asked for the family to come to her office, telling her that it was because of her mother's fears. In the office, Mrs. R. initially met alone with the worker while the children were in the agency's playroom. Mrs. R. acknowledged that she screamed a lot at all of her children but complained that with no husband to help her, she did not know any other way to get them to behave. The worker suggested to Mrs. R. that if she would ask the children to build a doll house together, then they could observe how things were when they played together. As Mrs. R. and the worker watched behind a one-way mirror, the children set about assembling the pieces of the doll house. As they observed, Eddie kept dropping pieces and stumbled on a toy, at one point. Mrs. R. became very upset and told the worker that he was just like his father who "never did anything right."

The structured observation provided an opportunity for the worker to help Mrs. R. recognize that the rage that she felt toward her husband was being directed at her son instead. Mrs. R. agreed that she always did this but said that she felt so help-less about her anger that she could not control herself. Plans were made to work further with Mrs. R. and her family so that she could find more appropriate ways to deal with her anger and so that Eddie could be relieved of feeling that setting a fire was the only means of expressing frustration.

In this structured observational interview, with the worker acting as a nonparticipant observer, the family subsystem could be seen operating with the one male isolated from the females in the family. The child who was ascribed the role of scape-goat carried out his tasks in a predictable way, continually attract-ing his mother's anger. The observation of the role performances and the relationship patterns provided for a point of entry into the system so that interventions could be planned to alleviate the extraordinary stresses felt by the mother and son and also to work toward restructuring the family.

It is desirable, whenever possible, to interview the total family for assessment purposes. Distortion of information is likely to be minimized with all family members present (Ander-son and Shafer, 1979). Observation provides an opportunity to see the interaction of the whole family system in a time of stress. When live reality is seen, discrepancies as to what actually is and what is said to be, are often found to be flagrant (Krill, 1968). Also, incongruencies between verbal and non-verbal messages can be observed.

An observational assessment tool of considerable value in obtaining objective type of behavioral data is the videotape. Increasingly, family therapists are videotaping interviews with families and then playing the tape back to them. This technique engages them in becoming researchers of their family system who are examining how they do, in fact, communicate with each other. Such observations can be extremely useful in identifying dysfunctional patterns of communication. In addition to feeding back what family members have said during a video-taped observation session, there are facial expressions, gestures, seating arrangements (and changes of seating), and postures that provide additional information about the family (Alger, 1976). Observations that are shared by the worker and the family members illustrate how the family functions, and enable the worker and the family to gain a clearer understanding of how problems develop and how they continue to be perpetuated. It should be noted that the use of videotaping in an observational session requires trust between the worker and the family. Therefore, it would be used only after a treatment contract had been agreed upon.

Although videotaping may be used in the home or office, efficient use of this technology usually takes place in office sessions. However, the simple home visit observation is a good substitute and has the advantage of observing the family in its natural environment. Home visits offer a unique opportunity for observing the physical setting as well as patterns of behavior and interactions among members of the family system. The home visit provides a means of seeing the living arrangements and of learning how family roles are enacted and tasks are performed. It is helpful in assessing a family to know who takes care of the baby, who assigns tasks, and who sees that they are carried out, as well as who sits in which chair and what significance there is to the seating arrangement. The home visit also may reveal information about linkages with other systems in the family's environment. For example, who answers the telephone? Do neighbors drop in? Are pictures of extended family members displayed? Are objects of religious significance in evidence? In addition, what does the home itself convey? Is it organized or chaotic? What impression do the furnishings convey about the family who lives there?

Visiting a home usually involves arrangements that are made in advance so that the family will feel it has been accorded respect. Experienced workers know that some resistant families fail to be at home at the appointed time or, if they are at home, they may have invited a neighbor or member of the extended family to help them feel more secure in the situation. Other families accept visits readily and show an aspect of their functioning that is different from what has been observed in the worker's office.

> A client who was seen initially in the worker's office appeared very uneasy as she discussed her family problems. Sitting on the edge of her chair, she kept her coat on and buttoned to the collar although it was warm in the office. Her discomfort in that situation was clearly observable. When she was visited by the worker in her home, there was a marked contrast in her manner. She was relaxed and lively as she prepared coffee in her immaculate kitchen.

The data provided by these observations suggest that this is a woman who takes pride in her home but who had difficulty in adapting to the unfamiliar, more formal surroundings in the worker's office. Such information is useful in assessing how well this client is likely to make use of resources where the surroundings are also unfamiliar and somewhat formal.

Before a worker makes a visit to the family home, it is important to know what information is being sought that the visit will provide. Prepared checklists and inventories are useful as guides to areas of functioning that can be observed in the home and will be discussed later in the chapter. If it is necessary for the worker to evaluate the physical environment, it may be helpful to study a checklist prior to the visit. Various categories of data are delineated in such areas as living space, furnishings, cleanliness, housekeeping. Becoming familiar with the categories of items to be observed will facilitate the process of focusing on needed data. A trained observer will take into account any unusual circumstances and differentiate them before making an assessment based upon observation. In times of crisis, some families become immobilized and cannot function at their usual level. A physically disorganized household may ordinarily reflect excessive overcrowding or may be due, in part, to badly neglected housing, but it also may be true that irresponsible housekeeping is due to the neglect of a parent who is overworked and overwhelmed or who is too ill to carry out household tasks. Assessment therefore must take into account the total family circumstances.

Observations of the social environment in the home reveal patterns of interactions that reflect the level and nature of the family functioning. Participant observers who have conducted studies of families where maltreatment is a problem have collected data that are useful for understanding and predicting dysfunction. Burgess and Conger (1978) compared such families with those having no history of this problem. Their findings, based on observations in homes, showed that there were lower rates of interactions among individuals in these families. Less verbal and physical interaction with children was observed, and parents were more likely to emphasize the negative in their relationships with them.

In violence-prone and apathetic families, parents have been observed to have distinctive patterns of communication. They were more unclear, had most topic changes, were highest on injunctions such as "behave yourself," and sought or shared little information. There was a high degree of interaction among the children and minimal interaction between the parents (Wells, 1981). Verbal accessibility, the readiness of families to communicate in words about important thoughts and wishes, has been observed as low in such families (Polansky, 1971). Wells believes this factor to be an indicator of capacity to engage in a process of change and therefore to be significant in assessment.

As an assessment method, observation has several limitations for human service workers. In some situations, the observer must obtain permission from the family to gain access for observation, as in visits to a home. Sanctions must also be granted, in some cases, for visits to institutional, work, or school settings before observation can take place. Also, the bias of the observer must be taken into account. Cultural and ethnic differences may present problems for observers who do not understand the implications of observed behaviors. For example, in some cultures making eye contact is deemed to be desirable and is interpreted as evidence of an honest, straightforward approach between people. In other cultures, however, it is customary and considered respectful for a child or young person to avoid eye contact with a parent or other person in a position of authority or respect.

Observation Exercise

You may become a more skillful observer by noting the physical environment at home. Which items in a room would convey useful information to an uninformed observer about the people who live there? What would an observer infer from seeing these items? Next, carry out this exercise at the work place in your own office and the office of colleagues. As you observe the physical environment, list the items that provide meaningful data about the occupant. After you have listed an item, write next to it what you would infer from observing that item.

Observations of the social environment can be similarly carried out. If you were observing a family on videotape or through a one-way mirror, what would you see? First, observe at home how the interactions between family members convey information about the family and its structure. What would you know its boundaries, the family roles and how they are performed? What the the patterns of communication? Observe who talks to whom and about what. Who makes decisions and who carries them out? Whose actions or comments provoke reactions from which other family members? How are the reactions acted out? Next, follow the same procedure at the work place and observe the patterns of people in that setting. What information would an observer infer from these patterns?

To apply these learnings to work with dysfunctional families, observe as many aspects of the physical environment as you can comfortably absorb. Note what you have absorbed and, at the end of the interview, record this data on an ecomap, genogram, or on a sheet of paper to insert in the case record. Follow the same procedures with the social environment, observing such nonverbal cues as gestures, posture, positioning, and affect, in addition to any other aspects of the transactions between family members that seem relevant to your assessment. Record pertinent data on the ecomap, genogram, or in the process recording in case record. When you have completed recording your observations, use the Evaluation of Assessment Method form at the end of this chapter to assess this method.

Checklist and Inventory

The checklist or inventory is a helpful assessment tool when it is used in conjunction with the family interview and direct observations. It helps to organize the mass of objective and subjective data collected by workers so that strengths or limitations in the family can be identified clearly. It may be used selectively at various stages in the assessment process to determine what is already known and what information remains to be collected. Prior to contact with the family, a checklist may be used to organize all of those data that have been entered in the records of the agency and in referral material from other sources. Information such as names, ages, occupations, place of residence, reason for referral, and source of referral may be entered as objective data. A checklist may also be used to list subjective information such as the nature of the family structure, how social roles are performed, and the patterns of communications. A comprehensive checklist will generally allow for data to be added as they are collected by the various methods discussed earlier. Table 5.1 is an example of such a checklist.

The worker will find a checklist or inventory is used according to the specific purposes to be achieved. At the outset they provide a means of studying what is known, and are a guide to the essential areas of information where concentrated effort must be expended. As the assessment process proceeds, they provide an orderly means of reviewing the accumulated data and are a reminder of gaps yet to be filled. Specific areas of concern can be highlighted with the worker's own symbols so that it is possible to red flag an area that must not be overlooked.

Inventories are useful for recording concrete data related to observations of the family home. The composition of a family is important when an inventory is used to determine whether the home provides a suitable living place since adequacy is dependent upon the number of people in the family, their sex, ages, and marital status. Knowledge about such facts as the number of rooms, beds per room, kitchen and bathroom facilities must be linked to the family composition. When examining a family and its physical environment, it is important to individualize families and take into account such factors as whether there is a handicapped person who must climb stairs. At the conclusion of an interview in which an inventory was taken of a household and its facilities, the data may be matched against predetermined standards for a family of that composition, or the worker may be required to make an independent assessment of whether living space is adequate to meet acceptable standards. If the worker is assessing whether the needs of an aged person are

TABLE 5.1

AREAS OF FUNCTIONING	(1) PRESENT LEVEL OF FUNCTIONING					(2) CHANGES IN FUNCTIONING SINCE CASE OPENING			(3) SERVICE PROVIDED	
	Adequate	Somewhat Inadequate	Grossly Inadequate	NA	UNK	Improved	No Change	Worse	Yes	No
I. Individual Functioning										
(A) *Mother (stepmother)*										
(1) Paternal functioning (care and training of children)										
(2) Marital functioning (affection and concern shown as wife)										
(3) Employment functioning (job stability, work patterns, and relationships)										
(4) Household functioning (adequacy of homemaking efforts or arrangements)										
(5) Physical functioning (illnesses and disabilities)										
(6) Emotional functioning (adjustment and behavior)										
(7) Use of formal resources (health, welfare, recreational)										
(8) Use of informal resources (friends, neighbors, extended family)										

being met in a geriatric facility, an inventory especially designed for that type of setting would be used, taking into account appropriate health and safety requirements of that age group. The level of functioning of family members may be evaluated according to these methods. Characteristics of each parent and child may be classified on forms according to physical, social, and emotional criteria, providing a means for the worker to assess each person's level of functioning. Table 5.1 is an example of a checklist. It shows areas of functioning of the mother or stepmother in a family. Functioning is examined according to present level of functioning or changes in functioning since case opening. Under the heading "Present Level of Functioning," ratings of adequate, somewhat inadequate, grossly inadequate, NA (not available), and UNK (unknown) are used. Under the heading "Changes in Functioning Since Case Opening," functioning is rated as improved, no change, worse. A third heading of "Service Provided" allows for yes or no to be checked. Eight areas of the mother's functioning are listed, beginning with parental functioning (care and training of children). Following this are marital functioning (affection and concern shown as wife), employment functioning (job stability, work patterns and relationships), household functioning (adequacy of homemaking efforts or arrangements), physical functioning (illnesses and disabilities), emotional functioning (adjustment and behavior), use of formal resources (health, welfare, recreational), use of informal resources (friends, neighbors, extended family).

When a checklist such as this is used by the worker, it provides a means of reviewing what is known about the mother's functioning, and this data can be recorded in a clear and easily readable manner. If in using the checklist the worker recognizes that a gap exists and that there is little or no knowledge about the mother's functioning in a specific area, then further information gathering may take place. For example, if you were assessing the capacity of a family to care for a physically handicapped child, data related to the physical functioning of the mother might be of particular significance. If, at the time of the assessment, you learn that the mother recently underwent a mastectomy, then in rating her present level of physical functioning you might check "somewhat inadequate" or "grossly inadequate," depending upon the circumstances. Several months later, your evaluation of the changes in functioning since the case opening would reflect whether her functioning had improved, had not changed, or was worse.

A number of other checklists or inventories are available. An inventory to be used in evaluating situations of neglect was developed by Norman A. Polansky and the staff at the University of Georgia Child Research Field Station (Popple et al., 1977). This Childhood Level of Living Scale investigates conditions of care under which children are reared and lists items related to physical care (safety, comfort, hygiene, and the like) and emotional/cognitive care (parental play with child, promoting curiosity, providing reliable role image, and so on).

Some agencies may find it necessary to develop an inventory in response to the needs of their particular clientele. An example would be an agency servicing physically handicapped children and their families. Such an agency would require that a checklist include emphasis on the special environmental facilities needed to enhance their clients' functioning. In an ecologically focused assessment, it would be necessary to know whether appropriate resources exist in the home, the school, and the community, and to evaluate how the family utilizes those that are available.

Checklist and Inventory Exercise

You may practice using a checklist or inventory at home and at work in order to become familiar with these assessment tools. When you have done this, begin to use them by selecting the appropriate tools for working with a specific family. After each usage, stop and think about whether it has been helpful. Has it helped to sharpen your focus on information still to be obtained? Compare your usual methods for dealing with data with your experience in using these methods. Are there advantages to the checklist or inventory? Are there disadvantages to the checklist or inventory? Evaluate this assessment method by using the Evaluation of Assessment Method form.

In order to learn how to use additional assessment tools, it is suggested that you read *Assessment Tools for Practitioners Managers, and Trainers* by Armand Lauffer (1982). In this volume, further uses of ecomapping are discussed, as well as task analysis, nominal groups technique, DELPHI, photography, gaming, and forcefield analysis.

Evaluation of Assessment Method

For the reader who is learning to use the assessment methods, it is worthwhile to consider how and where in one's own practice each method or combination of methods is most effective. In order to evaluate the utility of the method, the following format is suggested for use after each method has been tried.

(Name of Family)

(1) Date collected:

(2) Additional data needed:

(3) Advantages of this method:

(4) Disadvantages of this method:

(5) List other families in your caseload for which this method would have been helpful:

(6) Evaluation of assessment method:

__excellent __very good __good __fair __poor

Chapter 6

ASSESSING YOUR OWN CAPACITIES
TO DO ASSESSMENT

This chapter offers an opportunity to test one's own skill in making an ecologically based family assessment. A recognized method for reinforcing knowledge is to practice applying it in a simulated situation. For that purpose, a transcript of two videotaped interview vignettes is provided here. This transcript was developed by Anita Weinberg for learning purposes as part of the project Development and Delivery of Family-Centered Child Welfare Continuing Education Program by the Center for Social Work and Applied Social Research of Fairleigh Dickinson University. The videotapes were shown to experienced careworkers at the Family Counseling Service of Hackensack, New Jersey who, following each vignette, conducted a case conference to demonstrate how decision-making, utilizing information that had been gathered during the interview segment, is used in assessment and in the formulation of plans for intervention. The first interview depicts a mother who requests foster placement for the child. The second interview depicts a hospital social worker investigating suspected child abuse with the grandparents of an injured infant.

A framework for using the transcript as a self-teaching tool follows. It provides a step-by-step method for demonstrating whether the knowledge discussed in this volume has been integrated or whether further learning and practice are necessary for competence in carrying out a family assessment.

I.   Prepare to read the first interview, in which Mrs. Marsh discusses foster placement with the caseworker. Take into account concepts related to family systems, the family and its environment, and the family life cycle. Review, also, the methods suggested for use in assessment.

II. As you begin to read the interview, remember to note all pertinent data as it is revealed. Close the book at the end of the interview.

III. Stop and think. Select one or more assessment methods and begin the assessment process. Record what you have learned as a result of this interview on either an ecomap, genogram, or both. Use the following questions as a frame of reference.

1. What is the nature of the problem?
    a. What is its duration?
    b. Is it urgent?
    c. What actions have been taken by the client in the past?
    d. What was the client's response to this problem in the past?
    e. Are other family members involved? If so, what are their responses?
    f. What other systems are involved?
    g. How have they dealt with this problem in the past?
    h. What were the results of past actions?

2. What do you need to know about the family system?
    a. Who are the family members?
    b. What is the nature of the family's outer boundaries? Of the inner boundaries among family members?

3. What is the structure of the family in terms of:
    a. patterns of behavior
    b. patterns of communication
    c. role assignments:
        i. formal
        ii. informal
    d. role performances:
        i.   clarity
        ii. flexibility or rigidity
        iii. congruence or deviance

           iv. hierarchy respected or breached

           v. complementarity or lack of it

          vi. agreement or conflict

    e. family projection process or acceptance of one's responsibility for problems.

4. What do you know about the family's environment in terms of its relationship to these systems:

    a. extended family

    b. housing

    c. health care

    d. mental health

    e. work

    f. school

    g. legal institutions

    h. recreation

    i. community

    j. cultural or religious institutions

    k. friends

    l. social services

5. What stage in the family life cycle does the family occupy?

    a. What positions are occupied by its members?

    b. What developmental tasks are expectable for family members at this life stage?

    c. How are they meeting the expectations?

What do you know of family history in terms of the following:

    a. names and naming patterns

    b. ages

    c. occupations

    d. significant events such as birth, marriage, separation, divorce, illness, death

    e. ethnic background

    f. religious background

    g. relationship patterns, for example, closeness, conflicts, cut-offs

IV. Now that you have recorded all of the information that you recall from the interview, study each diagram and think about the areas in which there are serious gaps in data that must be filled before you can plan appropriate interventions. List these under the heading "data to be collected."

V. When you have carried out this part of the exercise, read the account of how experienced careworkers discussed the interview in terms of what information they had gathered and how they identified serious gaps in information prior to setting tentative goals.

    VI. When you have completed reading the account of the case conference, compare your approach to assessment with that of the caseworkers.

   VII. Examine data you collected and compare them with those identified by the caseworkers. List any data you did not record.

  VIII. Examine your list of those data to be collected and compare them with those identified by the caseworkers.

From what you have learned in carrying out this practice exercise, are there gaps in your learning that would benefit from reinforcement of knowledge? If so, turn to the appropriate section and review the relevant concepts about the family and assessment methods.

Carry out the same practice exercise with the second interview involving Mr. and Mrs. Pike, grandparents fo a child whose parents are suspected of physical abuse. Repeat steps I throught VIII.

Now that you have carried out two practice exercises using the concepts and assessment methods learned in this book, you are prepared to apply your knowledge to families in your own caseload. All of the concepts you have learned are generic and apply to every area of human services practice. Remember that as long as a family is active in your caseload, the assessment process must be ongoing with new data added as they accumulate.

Assessing a Family Interview

Interview 1

The following interview between a caseworker and a parent, Mrs. Marsh, takes place in the office of a child welfare agency.

Mrs. Marsh: How come Miss Burns isn't seeing me today?

Caseworker: Well, Miss Burns no longer works in this office. I'm Ms. Gilman and I'll be meeting with you about your request for foster care for Nicole.

Mrs. Marsh: I don't know what the big problem is. Miss Burns had all the information and she's always helped me before. Whenever I had to go to the hospital before, Miss Burns would arrange for Nicole to go to a foster home.

Caseworker: Well, I do know a good deal about you from Miss Burns. The reason I would like to talk to you is to inquire about your request for services.

Mrs. Marsh: I can't take it anymore—that's the problem. Everyone makes demands on me. The baby's always crying, my landlord wants his rent, the bills are piling up. Some days it is so bad I can barely get out of bed. I think I should go back to the hospital for a couple of weeks. My therapist thinks it would help. While I'm here, I would like you to arrange foster home placement for Nicole.

Caseworker: Well, you've come to this agency for help quite a number of times.

Mrs. Marsh: It's just me and Nicole—ever since I've had her it is very hard and nobody helps me. There is no one to depend on. I can't hold a job because of Nicole. Every time I get one, I get fired because I have to take off to take care of her and so we're on welfare. And that depresses me. When I get depressed, I like to go to the hospital. They understand me. I will feel better in a couple of weeks.

Caseworker: I understand that you and your husband are divorced. Do you see him often?

Mrs. Marsh: I am not divorced—I'm separated. I'd divorce him in a minute if I had the money. He doesn't do anything to help. All he does is criticize me. "You should have done this, you should have done that." If he knows so much about raising kids, why doesn't he take Nicole? You know that's not a bad idea. I should give Nicole to him. He wouldn't know what to do. The first day he had her he would dump her right on his parents.

Caseworker: Do you see your husband often?

Mrs. Marsh: About once a week. He's got a job, so he's pretty busy. His mother stops by sometimes to see us or take us out and see Nicole. She takes us shopping. She's really not too bad. At least she tries.

Caseworker: What about your family?

Mrs. Marsh: My family? Ha! I haven't seen them since I was 18 and that was four years ago.

Caseworker: What happened four years ago?

Mrs. Marsh: That's when I married James. They're so bigoted. Just because he's black. They said if I married him they never wanted to see me again. It wasn't because they didn't like him. He had a good job. In fact, better than my father's. It is just because he wasn't lily white, and anyway, what would the neighbors think?

Caseworker: Does your family know about the problems you and Nicole have been having?

Mrs. Marsh: Yes, they know. About six months ago Miss Burns, she asked me if I wanted to call them. I said "no way." I wasn't going to call them. So she asked if it were okay if she called. I said, "yeah." She didn't tell me the whole conversation, but the gist of it was that they didn't seem too concerned.

Caseworker: But your husband's family seems as if they were pretty interested.

Mrs. Marsh: I never considered it.

Caseworker: Well, is there any reason you haven't considered it?

Mrs. Marsh: I don't know if they really could take care of her and I don't like the neighborhood they live in. What's the problem? Why can't Nicole go into faster care like always?

Caseworker: Nicole has been in foster placement six times in the past two years. Mrs. Marsh, foster placement can be an extremely frightening experience. What I would like to explore with you is why you feel you can't take it any more and also explore the possibilities of you getting the help you need without having to go into the hospital and without having to leave Nicole.

Mrs. Marsh: My therapist feels I should go into the hospital.

Caseworker: If you like, I could speak to your threapist. Your emotional health is very important. But Nicole's emotional health is very important too.

Mrs. Marsh: Listen! I take good care of Nicole. Nobody helps me. No wonder I get sick with all I have to handle. I don't know why you are trying to make things so complicated. Why can't you arrange for a foster home for her? I'll be out of the hospital in a couple of weeks. What's the big deal? What is going to happen to her?

Case Discussion
Interview 1

Social workers in a child welfare agency meet in a case conference to discuss Mrs. Marsh's situation as presented in the interview with the caseworker.

Presenting Caseworker: I am bringing into supervision today a case of mine. Mrs. Marsh has now come back into the agency again requesting foster care for her preschool daughter, Nicole, temporarily while Mrs. Marsh goes back into the hospital. I have some concerns about this because we have been involved a number of times in the past with foster placement for Nicole, and I think it's time that we take a more careful look at this in terms of how to intervene this time. I think something different needs to be done this time. I also need some help in figuring out what is really going on here and I need some help in order to make an assessment at this point.

Supervisor: When you say "come back again," do you know how many times this has happened before and what were the circumstances in the past?

Presenting Caseworker: According to the records, it has been about 6 times prior to this request that previous workers have received placement calls, usually on a temporary basis, usually for two-three weeks while Mrs. Marsh goes into the hospital. She gets very depressed and overwhelmed and her therapist has often recommended hospitalization. Each time, we as an agency, have offered that as a solution.

Agency Director: So, in other words, what you are saying is that what appears to be a crisis each time is really a chronic condition.

Presenting Caseworker: That's what I think it is looking like.

Agency Director: Looking at it as a chronic condition, you can project that at this time there would be no substantial change without some new type of intervention.

Presenting Caseworker: I think so, and I think we should look at a new assessment and see how we could change our position as a child welfare agency.

Agency Director: Can you tell us about the family?

Presenting Caseworker: Yes, as much as I know about the family. Mrs. Marsh was married. She is currently separated from her husband. She was married four years ago. It is an interracial marriage. Apparently Mrs. Marsh's family "disowned" her at the point when she married her husband because of the racial situation, so, according to Mrs. Marsh, she has not had any contact with her own family. In terms of who is out there in a supportive system, as far as I know the only person that has been a supportive system to Mrs. Marsh was her mother-in-law. She visits on a weekly basis not only to help with Nicole but also to be supportive to Mrs. Marsh. Mrs. Marsh has mentioned she has taken her shopping, things like that. The father of Nicole also has been consistently involved. He visits once a week on a regular basis. What he is able to do, I really don't know.

Caseworker #2:   Each time Mrs. Marsh has requested foster care placement—did we ever contact any family members?

Presenting Caseworker: It doesn't appear that we did. In the past, we just met the request that she be placed in foster care.

Agency Director: So one of the missing items in the picture in making this assessment is who is Nicole's family—that it appears we have accepted Mrs. Marsh's statement that she is it and yet we have contradictory evidence.

Supervisor: I think the other piece we ought to know is what other support systems on a daily basis are available to this child. Presumably she is three or four years old. Is she in any kind of preschool program?

Presenting Caseworker: That is not clear at this point. It is really something I should explore. Nicole was in child care when Mrs. Marsh tried to hold down a job, but that did not work out when Nicole got sick and she would have to leave her job. But whether Nicole is currently in day care, I am not sure.

Supervisor: So what we are saying is that we have to look at this on a long-term situation, perhaps through school and adolescence. We have no indication that it will be otherwise and that Mrs. Marsh's way of getting time off is to be hospitalized. Has the agency been in contact with the therapist? Is there any way she could have permission to take an extended vacation besides going to a hospital on a long-term basis?

Caseworker #2:   I think it is important for her to have some time off. Being a single parent she becomes very overwhelmed with all the tasks that she needs to do on an everyday basis, and she needs to know that it is okay to have some other people available to help her and she doesn't have to go to the hospital every time.

Supervisor: This brings it to a full cycle as we explore more and more the support system that she has—the family support system—and consider this a chronic situation. At a reliable resource she may, in fact, feel less overwhelmed. I think our refusal as an agency in the past to label this chronic has contributed to making this necessary.

Caseworker #2:   I think it is good that this time you did not grant her foster placement immediately. This time as an agency, we began to take a different viewpoint. We are going to stick with it and see what she has going for her.

Agency Director: There are a number of questions.

Presenting Caseworker: The strengths of her and her systems.

Agency Director: Whatever family, whatever friends she may have. There is another system that needs to be explored in-depth. From what I am hearing it appears that we are the only crisis resource in the institutional system that supports Mrs. Marsh and Nicole. The hospital is one part. To what extent and how often she is an outpatient and when she should be admitted, etc., but certainly we have not dovetailed in our work up to now—it's been, one says, "Now it's time for you to come in," and another says, "Okay, I'm coming in," but there is no consistent support plan—the two need to be matched up and we don't know what other agencies are involved. We know Welfare is involved—there may be a day care center and there may be need for some other kind of supports that we haven't looked at.

We really don't know where to look until we have assessed what the strengths of the family network are. I think the important thing that is happening is that we really have looked at something and said it is not the kind of crisis that we thought it was previously.

What we don't know is whether it is in fact a crisis as well as a chronic condition because nobody has asked when she has to go into the hospital. Is it something that has to happen tomorrow, today, or next week, or if we were working on it could her psychiatric support system maintain her for a period of time?

Caseworker #2:   And even if it is a crisis, I think we are responding to it differently. We know that in a time of crisis, families respond most and we are saying that this may be a good time to begin to contact family members.

Supervisor: A good time to help Mrs. Marsh grow. We know from her history that she has a tendency when things go bad to cut people and other sources of help off and we have played into that by not helping her integrate her needs and her child's needs.

Presenting Caseworker: One of the questions I have, "Should I involve her mother-in-law in some kind of meetings to see what they could provide and her father also?" She does not seem receptive to that. She seems unable to see their involvement as helpful. She has a hard time asking directly for help.

Supervisor: We are going to create a crisis for her because in the past we have been so cooperative by moving Nicole in and out of foster home placement. She hasn't had to deal with the possibility of doing that.

Agency Director: We have responsibility here both to Mrs. Marsh and the child. First, to the child, since we are a child welfare agency, to intervene in a more constructive way based on an assessment that this probably is a long-range situation. We are going to look for the least disruptive way to intervene with as many of her well-known supports as possible. We have a responsibility to the whole family to support them as much as possible so that they can more and more take over that role for Nicole. We also have a responsibility to the rest of the service system of which we are a part. I think the first step is to alert the hospital and the therapist that we are in fact going to create a new crisis by not responding to the request simply by removing Nicole for a couple of weeks because we do not know what the fallout from that will be, and they need to be there to be supportive.

Presenting Caseworker: Guess I feel that. I think six placements is ridiculous.

Agency Director: Does that give you a sense of a direction?

Presenting Caseworker: I feel very good about it because, first of all, by giving a message to Mrs. Marsh that we see there is more than her involvement with Nicole. There is more to Nicole's family than just Mrs. Marsh and we are making a statement that we see that.

Agency Director: We are making a statement and in fact we are supporting the reality that the father is responsible.

Supervisor: We should come across as supportive to her and not blaming her.

Caseworker #2:   That's right. Otherwise you are going to have her right back where she was before and we are not saying she is inadequate, but in fact really is in need of what everyone else is in need of: supports available to herself and Nicole.

Agency Director: And that she hasn't had what is available, that is, all your resources.

Supervisor: She is quite right to be overwhelmed because no one has really helped her.

Supervisor: So, you think—contact the other agencies first—the hospital.

Agency Director: I am saying they are simultaneously involved, and we need to think of ourselves as part of the total system rather than isolated from them.

Supervisor: That this time around it is going to be felt like a crisis even though we are not labeling it a crisis. I think we have to understand that this time around even if the actual steps turn out to be the same; that is, if there isn't time enough to accomplish this before she does get hospitalized and Nicole does go into foster home placement, we still hopefully will have made a big difference by saying that this is not how we see it.

Agency Director: I think that says it all.

Interview 2

In the following interview, a child welfare worker meets with Mr. and Mrs. Pike, grandparents of a two-month-old child, to discuss possible child abuse, beginning the process of assessment in this case.

Caseworker: Mr. and Mrs. Pike, as you know, your grandson was admitted to the pediatric intensive care unit at Blair Hospital early this morning.

Mrs. Pike: I wish someone would let us know what is going on here. I went over to the hospital when my daughter-in-law called from there, but nobody would talk to me. We couldn't get any information about the baby. And now you're here. What's going on?

Caseworker: Your son and daughter-in-law brought the baby to the hospital stating that he fell off the table from his infant's seat while they were in another room. They were afraid he broke his arm.

Mr./Mrs. Pike: Is he okay?

Caseworker: The doctors found that he had indeed broken his arm. In fact, they discovered that there are three other broken bones in his body, apparently from other injuries.

Mr. Pike: What are you talking about?

Caseworker: The doctors found significant evidence of child abuse.

Mrs. Pike: But the baby is only 2 months old. Who could do that?

Caseworker: That's one of the questions I wanted to discuss with you.

Mrs. Pike: You don't think we hit the baby?

Caseworker: Your son and daughter-in-law live upstairs from you, is that correct?

Mr. Pike: Right, when they got married we gave them the apartment upstairs until they got on their feet.

Caseworker: So you see the baby often?

Mrs. Pike: Just about every day. What are you getting at?

Caseworker: Since you do see the baby so often and are the baby's grandparents, it's natural that I would want to see if you have any information about the baby's injuries. The doctors at the hospital have expressed great concern and feel that the evidence is overwhelming that the baby has been abused.

Mr. Pike: Abused, abused, you keep saying abused. By who? The baby is only 2 months old. Who would want to hit a little baby? He never looked like he was hurt to me. He cries alot, but what baby doesn't?

Caseworker: I met today with your son and daughter-in-law at the hospital earlier. They say they have no idea how the baby could have gotten those other broken bones.

Mrs. Pike: Maybe it's a disease. I read in a magazine where a family was charged with child abuse when the baby had a rare disease that caused the bones to break.

Caseworker: The doctors have investigated bone disease and so far have ruled out that possibility. They will be keeping the baby in the hospital for a short period of time to observe him and to allow time for all his injuries to heal.

Mrs. Pike: Then what happens?

Caseworker: At this point I'm not entirely sure. That's the purpose of an investigation. If there is a judgment of abuse, and in this case there appears to be substantial evidence to support such a judgment, then this agency will petition the court to remove the baby from its parents. This may be for either a short time period or permanently depending on the circumstances surrounding the case.

Mrs. Pike: Do Chris and Tony know this?

Caseworker: I explained it to them at the hospital.

Mr. Pike to Mrs. Pike: (Angrily) Do you understand what this woman is saying? First, she accuses this family of child abuse, and now she's threatening to take our grandson away. No way! We don't have to take this.

Mrs. Pike to Mr. Pike: Shush, let's just hear what she says.

Mrs. Pike to Caseworker: Look, we don't know anything about the baby being hurt. Chris and Tony are young. They're only 19 and 20. Maybe they made some mistakes. But we don't want this baby taken away.

Mrs. Pike to Mr. Pike: I'm not working. What do you think if we took the baby?

Mr. Pike: Sure, of course. Didn't I say that? What did you think I meant? I'm not letting any cocakmamie welfare agency take my grandson. No sir!

Caseworker: So you're interested in caring for the baby?

Mrs. Pike: Of course. Now, I'm not saying that the kids hurt the baby. But we want our grandson with the family.

Caseworker: Have you every heard any loud noises or screams from the baby in your house?

Mrs. Pike: Chris and Tony yell alot. It's just them. Look, they're young and they've both had problems. It's never been serious.

Caseworker: What sort of problems?

Mr. Pike: It was that damn school he went to and all those lousy kids he met there. They got him into trouble. He spent some time in reform school. Tony's a good kid. The same thing happened with my other boys and they're doing okay now. One owns a garage and the other works steady too. But Tony's a good boy, he'll straighten out. Getting married to that flake didn't help him any.

Mrs. Pike: Shush!

Mr. Pike: No, let the woman know. His wife is a looney. Since they've married they don't go out, they don't have friends. Niether of them work. All they do is watch TV. Day and night you hear it blaring.

Caseworker: How do you get along with them?

Mr. Pike: Fine. Tony's a good kid and we've always been close. I wish he'd get a job though. Staying in the house isn't good for anyone.

Caseworker: How often do you see your son and daughter-in-law?

Mr. Pike: Tony comes down every night when I get home from work. We usually have a beer or two together before dinner. The whole family—my other two sons and their families—come over for dinner on Sunday.

Mrs. Pike: There are twelve for dinner every Sunday. Our family is real close. Chris comes down most every day to talk too. She's had problems but she's a sweet kid. We're her only family (turning to her husband). She's a little afraid of you so she comes down when you're at work.

Mr. Pike: She's afraid of everything, that's her problem.

Mrs. Pike: Well, you don't help any. You snap at her every time she says something.

Caseworker to Mr. and Mrs. Pike: Okay. You stated earlier that you would be interested in caring for the baby. While I'm not certain that this is a possibility, I would like to explore this with you. It's been a long time since you had an infant to care for. I'd like you to think about the implications for your life of possibly raising another child.

Mrs. Pike: I don't see what the big deal is. I'm not so old. I'm only 46. I've raised three kids, so a fourth is nothing special. My kids all turned out Okay. I'm home all day anyway. So I'll give up bingo twice a week. We have lots of room.

Mr. Pike: Sure, I'm working most of the time. I drive a milk truck so it's really Betty who will care for the baby. He's our grandson and we're not letting any stranger take care of him.

Case Discussion
Interview 2

Continuing the assessment process, the caseworker meets in a supervisory case conference to discuss the Pike interview.

Agency Director: I'm glad your are bringing in the Pike family case for discussion today. This is one of those very difficult situations where it is so easy in terms of thinking "what do we do this minute" when a disaster goes on. While most of us are familiar with the general gross details of the case, I would be interested for you to tell us first what you have been able to assess without reviewing the facts that we really know.

Presenting Caseworker: In the interview with the grandparents— the Pikes—I feel they were very caring, concerned people. Okay, in this family there are Mr. and Mrs. Pike. Mrs. Pike is 46. They have three children. They have three sons. Tony has two older brothers, who are out of the household. I believe they have their own families. They do visit the family every Sunday for dinner. Tony is married to Chris. He is 19 and they have a 2-month old child who has been abused. My feeling is that even if they are caring and concerned and are all in the same house and see each other every day, it makes me think there is a real collusiveness that concerns me and I need help at this point in knowing what short range plans to make; how to test that out in order to make a more permanent plan for this 2-month-old child.

Supervisor: You're saying that you want to look at this in two stages, one short term and the other long term.

Presenting Caseworker: Yes, right now the baby is in the hospital. I don't know how long they will keep him there, but we need to make some plans soon and I would like to look within the family systems to see if there were any possibility of placing this child temporarily.

Agency Director: You keep by-passing the obvious, the grandparents, which leads me to believe that on some level you are not comfortable with this as a viable option.

Presenting Caseworker: Why I'm not so comfortable is because it seems the grandparents are very involved with the parents, Tony and Chris. I don't get a sense that they are that involved with the infant. It may be because Tony and Chris are so needy themselves. Tony has a very strong connection with his father and Chris with her mother-in-law. She visits every day and chats. I think that this is very positive. I don't know how comfortable I would feel placing the infant with the grandparents.

Supervisor: It seems like there isn't any room for the infant in that household.

Presenting Caseworker: In many ways Tony and Chris are still functioning as children in this household and have not been acting as parents.

Agency Director: Well, obviously no one has been acting as parents when you figure there are four broken bones in a 2-month-old baby. You average that out.

Presenting Caseworker: Also, neither of them is working. Living in Tony's parents' house, both of them home all day apparently very isolated from any contact with the outside world, peers and friends, etc.

Supervisor: So the fact is again in these horrendous cases, that this may be a very good time to get the family mobilized, to see what the extended family is and to see if there are support systems. I think there would be no automatic putting the baby back with the grandparents.

Presenting Caseworker: But the grandparents are very interested.

Agency Director: If I remember the facts, the grandparents kept saying, "We do not want the child raised by a stranger. We don't want that child out of our family." Has somebody really defined the family as something more than the four, and the baby five, people that live in one house?

Presenting Caseworker: I think that is important. Because there are other members. Tony has two brothers who also had problems when they were younger who straightened themselves out and are working the problems out. They are out of the household. Maybe they are functioning more as adults, more than Tony at this point in his life.

Agency Director: And they are parents.

Supervisor: We may not get as much opposition from the family as it looks like, because for some reason they are uncomfortable now with this environment for this child, now finally feeling it is a toxic environment because there is no particular reason they took the baby to the hospital because it has happened so many times before. They seem to be reaching outside this home.

Agency Director: We must really say that again. That's very important. These people have gone through periods of trouble in their lives. They themselves have identified it with their boys. There is some question about the outside intervention with Tony when he went to reform school if it was really effective in changing anything, but nontheless there have been other times in this family's life when they had to get things bad enough for other people to get in. You really do begin to wonder if that is why the parents took the child to the hospital with multiple fractures, which then makes you say not "we're going in to try to help them," but, in effect, "*they* did something to ask for help."

Supervisor: So we are back to the extended family, that possibly the grandparents are not the best people.

Agency Director: Wait a minute. We identified three children in this discussion: the baby, Chris, and Tony. And maybe what we are saying is if there were another place for the baby, maybe Tony and Chris could get something from being treated by his parents as children needing to learn to become adults—maybe—we don't know. And that's something you don't test out overnight.

Presenting Caseworker: There would be more space for that if the child was not in the same house.

Supervisor: But if you go back to your original idea of looking at this short term and long term, I think you have to say loud and clear that this is such an abominable life-threatening situation that there is no way, short term, that you put that baby back in that household until you had a better sense of what's going on.

Agency Director: The other side of that is, is there anything so gross in this family that one would rule out right now, looking at *ever* having that child return to that family?

Presenting Caseworker: Absolutely not. My feeling is that Tony and Chris are young parents and they still have a lot of things to work out for themselves, becoming adults, and that will take some time.

Supervisor: That is all in the area of the unknown and that is your long-term situation.

Agency Director: All right, now let's go back to short-term. Because we are saying perhaps in the long run this baby could be brought up within its family. Perhaps. Let me look at the short-term. We really don't know how much time we have before the hospital discharges the child. But again, consistent with our own policy of the least drastic intervention, it would be worth looking into the home of one of the other family members as a temporary placement.

Presenting Caseworker: I don't know much about them. I think that is something I should explore; their own environment, if they're working, whether they have children, how they are doing, whether they are working, and whether they could accept having the baby temporarily placed in their family. I think Tony and Chris and the grandparents would feel very good about that—much better than having the child removed from the family. They have made it very clear they do not want the child removed from the family.

Caseworker #2:   I think one thing we would learn is what is their capcaity to rally around as an extended family. This is the only way this family is going to make it. They really need to be taught skills on how to really use themselves as an extended family.

Supervisor: You are saying diagnostically that if they cannot respond to this initial piece, you have a pretty good idea that this family may not have the capacity to raise a child.

Presenting Caseworker: I think we are leaning more toward Tony's siblings. I think it is an important step for him to take at this point.

Agency Director: Let's get back to the parts of the story that are missing—at least his parents tell of his feeling that he has his brothers and sisters-in-law who are available to him as a resource. It is certainly something that needs to be looked at.

Presenting Caseworker: Yes.

Agency Director: Let's move on to one more thing quickly. If we run into either a concrete stumbling block in exploring that placement or another gut-level feeling such as you started with that this doesn't feel right, we still have to think of a temporary placement for this child. On the assumption that this type of family work takes quite a bit of time, what would be your recommendation?

Presenting Caseworker: I think I would like to meet with the Pikes further—especially the grandparents—and really get to know them better. Right now my gut feeling would be to look outside the family for something temporary—very temporary. With the grandparents and parents visiting and having a major involvement with the child. And giving some time to test out what their capacity is for nurturing and taking care of the child. And at some point looking for a long-term plan.

Agency Director: Okay, but we can predict something, too. If it came to that, an emergency placement outside the family, we would then be thinking in two stages beyond that—a placement in the family, as a second thing, and then eventually if that proved to be possible, return to the full control of the parents.

Supervisor: Just one note of caution. We see a lot of cases in this agency and it is unusual even in the worst cases to have a baby 8 weeks old who has multiple fractures. I would say this is rather a seductive family and this is a life-threatening situation and the assessment should be careful and objective and perhaps even two people involved in it because it is so easy to be hooked into a decision.

Caseworker #2:   Absolutely!

Agency Director: Look this decision-making that we are talking about today. What you are really saying is we go only so far as to say where should this baby be placed temporarily and then we need to get back here and really look at a solution.

Caseworker #2:   Absolutely. What we are saying is that I should first explore Tony's siblings and their families and see what is available there and then come back to the group and tell you what my assessment is.

Supervisor: One step before that. I think we are talking about temporary placement for this child in any case. Because as we were saying the assessment is on hold.

Agency Director: One more point before we end this. It isn't you who should explore the possibility of placement with one of the siblings, it's you and the family together. The one you are now in touch with. The more you involve them, the more you will have a chance to test it out.

Presenting Caseworker: I feel they will respond most by being involved in the process than by being left out.

Agency Director: You feel a little less uneasy.

Presenting Caseworker: It also feels good to bring it to a place.

Agency Director: We may have diffused the kind of pressure we may be under when we begin to get all the phone calls from the hospital, from the doctors, from the nurses, from the social workers who really want to be out of this situation. We are a step ahead at this point. Is there anyone else that you know in the community, any other agency that we should alert as we look ahead?

Presenting Caseworker: I can't think of any. That's the problem with an isolated family. There don't seem to be many resources.

Supervisor: It can be an isolated family or a secretive family, that is what we can find out.

Agency Director: I think we've gone as far as we can with this.

Presenting Caseworker: At some point, I'll get back to you again.

Narrator: An accurate family assessment is essential to developing realistic treatment plans. This videotape demonstrates how a family assessment is developed from information gained in client interviews. The family systems model used is applicable for work in the child welfare agency and is a useful tool for making realistic treatment plans.

Chapter 7

RELATING ASSESSMENT TO INTERVENTION

The goal of an ecological approach to family assessment is to pave the way for planning appropriate interventions to help a troubled family. When based upon sound knowledge of how the family system functions, how the family relates to its environment, and what stage the family occupies in its life cycle, the worker is prepared with a broad grasp of those factors that contribute to the family's problems. To carry out the family assessment, as described in this book, the worker and family members collaborate in examining unmet needs. Drawing upon one or more of the array of assessment tools for use in the focused interview (e.g., ecomap, genogram, family sculpture), they are engaging in a productive relationship.

In the process of sharing information and discussing the nature of the problem, family members usually express how they want to be helped. In doing so, both short-term and long-term goals are identified as a means of bringing about change. Whenever possible, interventive strategies are planned as a joint undertaking. Generally, this approach is enhanced by the spirit of trust and cooperation that characterizes the effective helping process.

The very nature of the assessment method used sets the tone for the interventions and interactions that follow. As a result, the worker is in a position to evaluate interventive choices with an understanding of which is most appropriate for a family. Change may be planned for the family system, the family's environment, or both. The capacity of the worker to help with change must be a realistic consideration. Working together, the family gains a sense of the worker's capacity to understand their problems and to plan for feasible goals.

If the family's ecomap has shown a scarcity of resources in their environment, then interventive plans are made to include a survey of possible people and institutions who are available to provide help. This is followed by the active linking of resources to the family. The evaluation of a family's capacity to reach out to a person or institution to ask for and accept help is an important step in a thorough assessment. In some families, simply offering a referral to a resource is adequate assurance that it will be utilized, but in other families, direct involvement on the part of the worker is required to bring about the linkage and to sustain ongoing utilization.

When a family's genogram shows a history of problems over three generations, as in a family with a pattern of alcoholism, the shared experience promotes recognition of the pattern. Planning how to deal with the problem follows naturally in a collaborative undertaking so that working toward accepting responsibility for change on the part of the family members is an outgrowth of the shared assessment. Similarly, when family events are recorded on the genogram, the consequences of "off-time" events, such as an early parental death, are examined jointly and lead to understanding of how this has affected family members. Identification of "cutoffs" from significant members is another characteristic of dysfunctional families that shows up on geograms. Recognition of the phenomenon leads to discussion of how it can be approached and resolved. Interventions to deal with genogram findings take place in an atmosphere of mutual understanding of family dynamics and so are likely to result in mutually planned interventions.

Family sculpture as a shared experience also promotes a recognition of family dynamics. Creating awareness in the particpants that scapegoating is taking place or that overinvolvement results in dysfunction is a constructive move toward intervention when it evolves in an atmosphere of trust. Suggestions to deal with these problems in terms of short-term and long-term goals are acceptable in a positive environment.

Throughout the assessment, observation is an inherent part of the process of preparing the worker to recognize how strengths or limitations in the family system are demonstrated. Astute observation gives the worker a basis for deciding whether the family can be mobilized to act on its own behalf or whether it must receive considerable support to move ahead. In the office interview or at home, the family shows by its behavior how it copes with stress. This provides the worker with a means of gauging the family's capacity for meeting new situations so that interventive plans can reflect the observations. Further evaluation of strengths or limitations in the family system or family environment follows the assessment of data collected by means of checklists or inventories. This approach, when combined with observation, identifies how interventive planning can be responsive to family needs.

Human service workers who have expanded their perspective of family functioning and who have collaborated with families in carrying out the assessment process are well equipped to proceed with the helping process. Assurance that their knowledge and mastery of family assessment will lead to worthwhile interventive plans promotes confidence in professional accomplishment.

REFERENCES

Alger, Ian (1976) "Integrating immediate video playback," in P. J. Guerin (ed.) Family Therapy: Theory and Practice. New York: Gardner Press.

Anderson, Lorna M. and Gretchen Shafer (1979) "The character-disordered family: a community treatment model for family sexual abuse." American Journal of Orthopsychiatry 49 (July).

Beal, Edward W. (1980) "Separation, divorce and single-parent families,'" in E. A. Carter and M. McGoldrick (ed.) The Family Life Cycle: A Framework for Family Therapy. New York: Gardner Press.

Biddle, Bruce J. and Edwin J. Thomas (1966) Role Theory: Concepts and Research. New York: John Wiley.

Boehm, Bernice (1967) "Protective services for neglected childred," in Social Work Practice: Proceedings of the National Conference on Social Welfare. New York: Columbia University Press.

Bowen, Murray (1978) Family Therapy in Clinical Practice. New York: Jason Aronson.

Brill, Naomi I. (1978) Working with People: The Helping Process. Philadelphia: J. B. Lippincott.

Burgess, Robert L. and Rand D. Conger (1978) "Family interaction in abusive, neglectful and normal families." Child Development 49 (December).

Carter, Elizabeth A. and Monica McGoldrick (1980) The Family Life Cycle: A Framework for Family Therapy. New York: Gardner Press.

Compton, Beulah Roberts and Burt Galaway (1979) Social Work Processes. Homewood, IL: Dorsey Press.

Derdyn, Andre P. (1977) "Child abuse and neglect: the rights of parents and the needs of their children." American Journal of Orthopsychiatry 47 (July).

Dukette, Rita, R. Born, B. Gagel, M. Henricks (1978) Structured Assessment: A Decision-Making Guide for Child Welfare. Washington, DC: Department of Health, Education and Welfare.

Duvall, Evelyn M. (1977) Marriage and Family Development. Philadelphia: J. B. Lippincott.

Erikson, Erik (1963) Childhood and Society, New York: W. W. Norton.

Germain, Carel B. and Alex Gitterman (1980) The Life Model of Social Work Practice. New York: Columbia University Press.

Goldstein, Joseph, Anna Freud, and Albert Solnit, Jr. (1973) Beyond the Best Interests of the Child. New York: Free Press.

Hadley, Trevor R., T. Jacob, J. Milliones, J. Caplan, Jr., and D. Spitz (1974) "The relationship between family developmental crises and appearance of symptoms in family members." Family Process 13 (2).

Haley, Jay (1973) Uncommon Therapy: The Psychiatric Techniques of Milton H. Erickson, M.D. New York: W. W. Norton.

Hartman, Ann (1979) Finding Families: An Ecological Approach to Family Assessment in Adoption. Beverly Hills, CA: Sage.

———(1978) "Diagrammatic assessment of family relationships." Social Casework 59 (October).

Hollis, Florence (1972) Casework: A Psychosocial Therapy, New York: Random House.

Kadushin, Alfred (1980) Child Welfare Services. New York: Macmillan.

Keniston, Kenneth and the Carnegie Council on Children (1977) All Our Children: The American Family Under Pressure. New York: Harcourt Brace Jovanovich.

Krill, Donald F. (1968) "Interviewing as an intake diagnostic method." Social Work 13 (April).

Lauffer, Armand (1982) Assessment Tools for Practitioners, Managers, and Trainers. Beverly Hills, CA: Sage.

Minuchin, Salvador (1974) Families and Family Therapy. Cambridge, MA: Harvard University Press.

Neugarten, Bernice L. (1976) "Adaptation and the life cycle." Counseling Psychologist 6 (1).

New York Times (1981a) "Schools stereotype children with one parent." February 2.

———(1981b) "U.S. Census Bureau says divorce and unmarried couples increase in 1970s." October 18.

Nye, F. Ivan and Felix M. Berardo (1973) The Family: Its Structure and Interaction. New York: Macmillan.

Ogden, Gina and Anne Zevin (1976) When a Family Needs Therapy. Boston: Beacon Press.

Papp, Peggy, Olga Silverstein, and Elizabeth Carter (1973) "Family sculpting in preventive work with well families." Family Process 12 (June).

Perlman, Helen Harris (1961) "The role concept and social casework: some explorations." Social Service Review 35 (December).

Pincus, Allen and Anne Minahan (1973) Social Work Practice: Model and Method. Itasca, IL: F. E. Peacock.

Polansky, Norman A., R. D. Borgman, C. de Saix, and D. Sharlin (1971) "Verbal accessibility in the treatment of child neglect." Child Welfare 50 (June).

Polansky, Norman A., M. Chalmers, F. Buttenweiser, and P. Williams (1979) "Isolation of the neglectful family." American Journal of Orthopsychiatry 1 (January).

Popple, Philip R., C. T. Cruthirds, P. D. Kurtz, and R. Williams (1977) A Training Guide on Working with Parents Who Neglect Their Children. Nashville: University of Tennessee, Vantage Point Series.

Report of the Child Welfare Learning Laboratory, University of Michigan School of Social Work (1975) Family Assessment: A Self-Instructional Guide. Washington, DC: Social Rehabilitation Service.

Rhodes, Sonya L. (1977) "A developmental approach to the life cycle of the family." Social Casework 58 (May).

Schubert, Margaret (1971) Interviewing in Social Work Practice. New York: Council on Social Work Education.

Sgroi, Suzanne (1982) Handbook of Clinical Intervention in Child Sexual Abuse. Lexington, MA: D. C. Heath.

Solomon, Michael A. (1973) "A development conceptual premise for family therapy." Family Process 12 (2).

Stein, Theodore, Eileen D. Gambrill, and K. T. Wiltse (1978) Children in Foster Homes: Achieving Continuity of Care. New York: Holt, Rinehart & Winston.

Terkelsen, Kenneth G. (1980) "Theory of the family life cycle," in E. A. Carter and Monica McGoldrick (eds.) The Family Life Cycle: A Framework for Family Therapy. New York: Gardner Press.

Tomm, Karl and Maureen Leahey (1980) "Training in family assessment: a comparison of three teaching methods." Journal of Marital and Family Therapy 6 (October).

Tucker, Samuel (1979) "Minority issues in community mental health," in B. R. Compton and B. Galaway (eds.) Social Work Processes. Homewood, IL: Dorsey Press.

U.S. Bureau of the Census (1981) "Marital status living arrangements: March 1980." Current Population Reports: Population Characteristics. Series P-20, No. 365. Washington, DC: Government Printing Office.

Wallerstein, Judith S. and Joan Berlin Kelly (1980) Surviving the Breakup: How Children and Parents Cope with Divorce. New York: Basic Books.

Wells, Susan J. (1981) "A model of therapy with abusive and neglectful families." Social Work 26 (March).

ABOUT THE AUTHOR

Adele M. Holman, DSW, is a clinical social worker specializing in family therapy who has served since 1981 as a consultant to the Child Welfare Project of the Center for Social Work and Applied Social Research of Fairleigh Dickinson University, where her monograph "Family Assessment: An Approach to Child Neglect and Abuse" was published in 1982. She also conducts training for case managers and supervisors of the New Jersey Department of Human Services Division of Youth and Family Services in family assessment and intervention and recently conducted a series of workshops for day care teachers and administrators in working with dysfunctional families.